TRACES OF OZARKS PAST
Outlaws, Icons, and Memorable Events

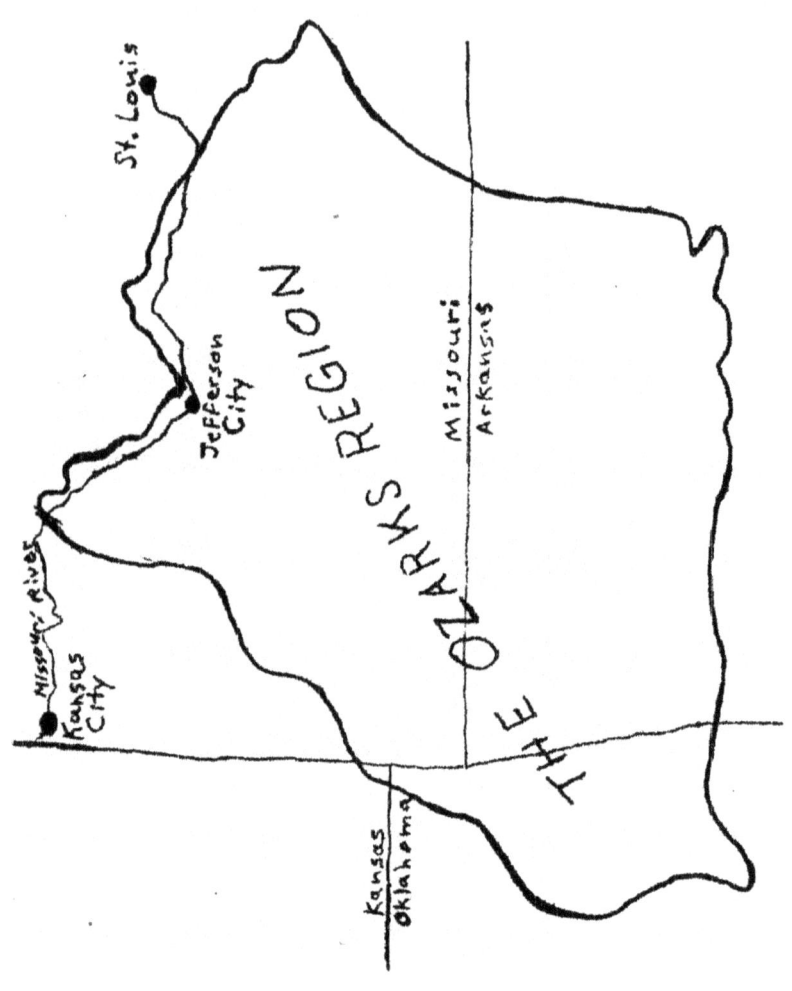

The Ozarks region.
(Illustration by the author.)

TRACES OF OZARKS PAST

Outlaws, Icons, and Memorable Events

Rex T. Jackson

HERITAGE BOOKS
2013

HERITAGE BOOKS
AN IMPRINT OF HERITAGE BOOKS, INC.

Books, CDs, and more—Worldwide

For our listing of thousands of titles see our website at
www.HeritageBooks.com

Published 2013 by
HERITAGE BOOKS, INC.
Publishing Division
5810 Ruatan Street
Berwyn Heights, Md. 20740

Copyright © 2013 Rex T. Jackson

Heritage Books by the author:
A Trail of Tears: The American Indian in the Civil War
James B. Eads: The Civil War Ironclads and His Mississippi
The Sultana Saga: The Titanic of the Mississippi

All rights reserved. No part of this book may be reproduced or transmitted in any form or by any means, electronic or mechanical, including photocopying, recording or by any information storage and retrieval system without written permission from the author, except for the inclusion of brief quotations in a review.

International Standard Book Numbers
Paperbound: 978-0-7884-5520-9
Clothbound: 978-0-7884-9055-2

TRACES OF OZARKS PAST
Outlaws, Icons, and Memorable Events

Rex T. Jackson

CONTENTS

1... "Arkansas Tom's" Last Roundup
9... 1904 St. Louis Excursion Train Disaster
19... Mathias Splitlog: "Millionaire Indian" of the Ozarks
27... Outlaw Henry Starr
33... Stand Watie: "Red Fox" of the Confederacy
47... "Officer Down": Hate Crimes in 1903 Joplin
55... Dancing into Eternity: Disaster at the Old Shrine Hall
61... 1917 Newton County Bank Robbery
65... Civil War Bushwhackers in Stone County
71... Kel-Lake Motel: An Icon of Route 66
77... "Oklahombres" Chieftain Bill Doolin
85... Battle at Keetsville: Blockade Hollow
91... War Eagle Mill
97... Granby Mining "Stampede"
105... Zagonyi's Brave Springfield Cavalry Charges
109... Tomahawking and Scalping in the Ozarks
117... Capturing Neosho: Secession in the Ozarks
123... Vigilante Lynching in the "Queen City of the Ozarks"

PREFACE

America's Ozarks region of Kansas, Oklahoma, Missouri, and Arkansas has hosted its share of our national heritage. Throughout time, over ancient traces and trails to modern roads of travel, each generation has made their contribution along the way.

Every region of the country has its own heroes and villains. Their accomplishments and activities so significant or so newsworthy, that they warrant further or continued study and research in order to ascertain the truth or gain understanding or full appreciation.

There has also been a number of devastating disasters that have been so heartrending that they draw us into their memorable, unforgettable grasp and gain our undivided attention—not letting go. It is to these things that beckon to us which peaks our interest, forces respect and captivates us.

The vastness of history is accessible by a broad, wide road where we can cruise back in any direction and delve into its rich bounties. The tales are seemingly endless, as each generation adds its own historic layer to the last.

In this small volume is only a trace amount of colorful Ozarks past. It is a noteworthy, historical collection of some of the persons, places, and events that have helped to mold and shape our nation's character. RTJ x

TRACES OF OZARKS PAST
Outlaws, Icons, and Memorable Events

2 BELIEVED SHOT IN GUN BATTLE WITH CITIZENS

Burglar Alarm Sounds in Three Stores and Merchants Fire on Robbers, One of Whom Staggers to Car—Another Seen to Collapse as Gang Speeds Away—Obtained Between $1,200 and $1,500.

Special to The News Herald.

Asbury, Mo., Nov. 26.—Five bandits in a motor car held up the Bank of Asbury at 2:30 o'clock this afternoon and escaped with between $1,200 and $1,500 in cash after engaging in a street fight with citizens. Two of the bandits are believed to have been wounded.

The bandit car, carrying the wounded men, dashed out of town, going west and was hotly pursued by several carloads of citizens heavily armed.

Headlines from the Joplin *News Herald*, Nov. 26, 1923.

"Arkansas Tom's" Last Roundup

THE TRACKS and trails of the past have left a lasting impression upon the Ozarks landscape. From Native Americans to the first white settlers who made it their homeland, much has transpired within its hills, hollows and prairies. The settlement of the region has been an ongoing journey, and through it all many of those who participated have left their footprints scattered along the traces of Ozarks history. These pathways have meandered in many directions, but they have all led to the present.

The Old West, for example, spawned its share of outlaws, due in large part to the post-Civil War and Reconstruction period, hard times, lack of law enforcement and other factors. Much of the lawless activity occurred in Indian Territory (Oklahoma) where scores of criminal-minded souls migrated—or, at times, took sanctuary, like Belle Starr, Frank and Jesse James, Bob, Jim, and Coleman Younger, Bill, Bob, Grat and Emmett Dalton, and Bill Doolan to name a few.

There were many other rough and rugged characters in the Nations who found employment on big ranches as cowboys; however, after Indian Territory was opened to homesteaders in April, 1889, the "land run" brought an end to the large ranches in favor of many smaller ones, which left many of the rancheros without a job. As a result, many of these cowboys who didn't want to get tied-down and own their own acreages, took to the Owl Hoot

TRACES OF OZARKS PAST

Trail and eventually a number of them became desperadoes or wound up in infamous outlaw gangs—rustling cattle, holding up trains, robbing banks and a host of other unsavory things.

Much of the taming of the West is attributed to gun-totting individuals, mass migration and the expansion of the railroad. Settling it was not for the weak or faint-hearted and the number of those that perished during this time, for one reason or another, will probably never be discovered.

Along with the ever-increasing population of the West came law and order, to some degree, but the fine line between a Western lawman and an outlaw was sometimes blurred—many gun slinging officers were known to be on both sides of the law. There was plenty of crime to go around during this wild and wooly time of the American West, and one of the last notorious outlaws to come out of this historic period would make his last stand in the Ozarks.

Roy Daugherty was born in Barry County, Missouri in 1870. Roy was said to have been raised, ironically, in a very religious family; his two brothers would go on to become ministers. Growing up in the hills and vales of the Ozarks, his life was hard and simple and he dreamed of something bigger, better and more exciting. When Roy became 14-years-old he left his hilly, rugged homeland and traveled west to Indian Territory and the big "spreads" that made up the western part of that country. Roy landed a job as a ranch hand and, for some reason, possibly wanting to leave his past behind or impress others, adopted the colorful name "Arkansas Tom" (some accounts say "Arkansas Tom Jones"). While serving as a cowboy in the Nations he met many cohorts that would later go on to become outlaws and members of various gangs who would ride the razor's edge, such as William M. "Bill" Doolin's gang called the "Oklahombres."

After the Oklahoma land run, Arkansas Tom lost his job and set his sights on a criminal lifestyle and teamed up with the Doolin Gang who knew of the planned, upcoming two-bank robbery attempt by the Daltons at Coffeyville, Kansas, on October 5, 1892— where only one of five survived. A few months after this, Daugherty would take part in one of the most historic shootouts to occur in Oklahoma between lawmen and outlaws at the small town of

"Arkansas Tom's" Last Roundup

Ingalls, which had about 150 residents; the town was named after Senator John J. Ingalls of Kansas.

Ingalls was located about nine miles east and one mile south of present-day Stillwater, Okla., in Payne County. It was a well-known hangout where a number of criminals were known to "hole up". There was a hotel, a couple of saloons and a gambling house to keep the riff-raff entertained.

On September 1, 1893, Ingalls was inhabited by such men as: Bill Doolin, "Bitter Creek" Newcombe, Bill Dalton, William "Tulsa Jack" Blake, Dan "Dynamite Dick" Clifton, George "Red Buck" Waightman, Charley Pierce—and, of course, Arkansas Tom—they were sometimes referred to as the "Wild Bunch."

Responding to a string of robberies, U.S. marshals and an assortment of lawmen loaded into a couple of Trojan-style horse-drawn wagons and were hot on the trail of the outlaws. Among the lawmen in pursuit was: E.D. Nix, Dick Speed, Tom and Ham Hueston, Henry Keller, George Cox, M.A. Ianson, James Masterson (Bat Masterson's brother), John Hixson, Ike Steel, Doc Roberts and others.

A blazing gun battle ensued at Ingalls and Arkansas Tom provided cover-fire for his companions from the second floor of the hotel, reportedly, killing Dick Speed and a man named Dell Simmons. The outlaws eventually fled the town galloping away from the hot, pouring lead, but Arkansas Tom was captured. He would be convicted of murder and sentenced to 50 years in prison as a result of the Battle of Ingalls. The other desperadoes would not live to see the turn-of-the-century—they were all hunted down and killed not long after the event.

In 1910, after 17 years of incarceration, Arkansas Tom was paroled and he returned to Oklahoma and attempted to go "straight" working in a café in the hamlet of Drumright, located west of Tulsa in present-day Creek County. This sort of ordinary lifestyle did not satisfy the restless heart of Arkansas Tom and he eventually came home to his native Missouri Ozarks and his life of crime.

In 1917 he was arrested for a series of daring bank robberies in Missouri—at Fairview, Oronogo and Wheaton. As a result, Arkansas Tom would do a few more years in an Oklahoma penitentiary for his lawlessness—he was paroled again on November 11, 1921.

Not long after his release he was at-it-again, this time helping to rob a bank. At 2:30 on the afternoon of November 26, 1923, the Bank of Asbury, Missouri, was robbed by four bandits. Two of the robbers entered the bank and one of them forced Cashier S. A. White and a clerk, Miss Lillie Coddering, at gunpoint "...into the vault and locked the door while the other scooped up all [the] cash in sight. The money was put into a bag," according to the Joplin *News Herald*.

Cashier White, using a burglar alarm that was inside the vault, alerted the businesses that were located across the street. P. Ytell, a garage owner, Charles Keer of the grocery store, and R. C. Coleman who was the town's pharmacist, met the bandits with gunfire as they darted out of the bank. The *News Herald* cried: "The bandit car, carrying the wounded men, dashed out of town, going west and was hotly pursued by several carloads of citizens heavily armed.

"The holdup was staged in a spectacular manner and was witnessed by a score or more of citizens, who began raining the bandit car with bullets soon after it was halted in front of the bank."

The bandits returned fire but their bullets missed their mark. The *News Herald* reported the action: "Gun play and bold acts of banditry that would rival some of the daring works of outlaws in the days when the James boys terrorized Missouri figured in the escape of the desperadoes."

Citizens pursued the spending get-a-way car vigorously, engaging them in three gun battles as they drove along. At one point, wrote the *News Herald* the day after the robbery, "Two of the outlaws got out on the running boards of their car and fired repeatedly at their pursuers." It was like a scene out of a Hollywood movie.

Eventually, Joplin police joined the hunt: Detectives Jess Laster, Demp Southard, Len VanDeventer and Tom DeGraff. A motorcycle patrolman, Clarence Allison, finally overtook the fleeing bank robbers near Crestline, Kansas—they had gotten their car bogged-down on a muddy road.

The bandits abandoned their vehicle and took to the woodlands

"Arkansas Tom's" Last Roundup

that bordered the road. In the meantime, however, Patrolman Allison had forsaken his "ride" as well and made his way around his prey and waited for them in a ravine. When three of them arrived he stepped out, not knowing where the fourth bandit was and ordered them to drop their weapons. The Joplin *Globe* reported: "Two of them carried rifles and the third a Luger automatic pistol."

As Allison made his way with his prisoners at gunpoint, he suddenly felt a weapon at *his* back and found the forth bandit—the "tables were turned" and he was now the prisoner!

They all marched back to the road where the outlaws commandeered another vehicle belonging to J.A. Lucas of Columbus, Kan., who was with his wife and son. Leaving Lucas and his family, they took the auto and forced Patrolman Allison to do the driving.

The tour took the bandits through the Kansas streets of Galena and Baxter Springs, Commerce, Okla., and through the "Devil's Promenade" (also known as "Spook Light") located along the border of Missouri. Here they dumped off Allison and sped on to the safety of the hills and hollows of the Ozarks. About the cruise through the streets of Galena, Baxter Springs, and Commerce, the *News Herald* had this to say: "There were side curtains on the bandit car and pedestrians on the streets did not know what was going on. They drove slowly through the streets."

Left behind in their original car were two sacks of silver that amounted to about $100. It was later ascertained that the heist yielded a total of $1,088 of cash to split between them. Allison later reported that he did not believe that any of the robbers were seriously wounded during the whole affair.

It would take several months but the law would finally catch up to one of the notorious bandits in Joplin, Mo., at a house at 1420 West Ninth Street. On August 16, 1924, Roy Daugherty, "...alleged slayer of eighteen men," (during his lawless career) according to the Joplin *Globe* published the next day, was killed by detectives and his body riddled by bullets.

Apparently, Detective Chief William F. Gibson had went around to the back of the house where Daugherty was hold up, he "...stepped on the rear porch...to cut off escape" and a bullet was

TRACES OF OZARKS PAST

fired that took "...a generous clip out of the officer's straw hat." Detective Gibson returned the favor and three of his four shots hit their mark. Daugherty somehow made his way to another room of the residence where he was met by Detective Len VanDeventer who had come in through the front door. Finding the armed, wounded outlaw, VanDeventer discharged his weapon delivering the fatal shot just above the outlaw's heart—he died almost instantly; there had been a total of eight shots fired during the gunfight. The owner of the house, "Red" Snow, was not present at the time, but his wife, 12-year-old daughter and baby were in the house but somehow were unharmed during the action.

The body of Roy "Arkansas Tom" Daugherty was taken to the Hurlbut Undertaking Company—where, according to the Joplin *News Herald* dated August 18, 1924, "Approximately 5.000 persons, men, women and children, filed through the morgue...to view the body of Roy Daugherty, notorious bank bandit and alleged killer...Most of the thousands who gazed upon the pallid face were merely curious to view a man known to be of the type of fearless desperadoes who robbed, plundered and killed in the early days of outlawry when gun play was not uncommon. They knew that few of his kind have survived."

In Daugherty's final throes of life, the 54-year-old public enemy lived long enough to learn an important lesson: crime does not pay. However, the young Ozark boy who dreamed of bigger and better things for himself as a ranchero in the Wild West may have found just what he was searching for when this cowboy-turned-outlaw finally joined the Last Roundup—his trail had ended.

Bibliography

Jackson, Rex T., *Roy "Arkansas Tom" Daugherty's Last Roundup*, Vol. 8, No. 1, The Ozarks Reader Magazine, Neosho, Missouri, 2011.

McNab, Chris, *Gunfighters: The Outlaws and Their Weapons*, Thunder Bay Press, San Diego, California, 2005.

Turner, George, *Gun Fighters*, Baxter Lane Company, Amarillo, Texas, 1972.

Other Sources

Joplin *News Herald*, November 26, 27, 28, 1923
Joplin *Globe*, November 27, 1923
Joplin *News Herald*, August 18, 1924
Joplin *Globe*, August 17, 19, 1924

Two young female victims of the train wreck, Dicy Ream and Gertrude Loud, at rest in the Worsley Cemetery located near Bronaugh, Mo. The girls were twelve years old at the time of the St. Louis Excursion Train disaster. The beautiful headstone was made in Italy.

1904 St. Louis Excursion Train Disaster

OVER THE YEARS the people of the Ozarks have endured their share of disasters – floods, tornadoes, fires, explosions, collisions and many other things. When tragedy strikes, however, the results are always the same: dealing with the injured, the clean-up and aftermath as well as cause and prevention. The railroads were no exception and during the mid-1800s to the early part of the 20th century there were many catastrophes that came to haunt the tracks. During this steam-powered era, America experienced a boom of steel rails that crisscrossed the landscape and enabled many passengers and freight to be transported to many destinations; but on occasion, unfortunately, traveling the rails also became a roadway of sorrows.

In 1904 excursion trains brought scores of sightseers to St. Louis, Missouri from around the world, across the nation and the Ozarks. They came to see the St. Louis World's Fair (Louisiana Purchase Exposition), and celebrate the 100th anniversary of the Louisiana Purchase.

The Exposition took several years to prepare due to a massive amount of construction. It required over 10,000 workers to turn more than 1,200 acres of tangles and swampland in Forest Park and Clayton into a grand place of buildings, avenues, gardens and waterways. Over 20 million fairgoers came to marvel at "living" displays, science exhibits, art, industry and over 500 vendors scattered over the fairgrounds – selling and launching new products. There were many nations that utilized the St. Louis World's Fair and gave visitors a chance to see things they had never seen before.

The Louisiana Purchase Exposition also hosted the 1904 Olympic Games, which took place from August 29 to September 3 at Francis Field. The World's Fair had something for everyone and the railroad was one of the best modes of transportation to get there.

One such rail service that offered attractive rates and crammed their cars to capacity was the Missouri Pacific Railroad, which was making a run from southeast Kansas and southwest Missouri to the St. Louis World's Fair. According to the Warrensburg *Weekly Standard-Herald* the Missouri Pacific World's Fair "special" was "made up at Wichita, Kansas, and run on what is called the south branch of the Missouri Pacific to Pleasant Hill [Missouri] where it takes the main line east to St. Louis."

A passenger of that Missouri Pacific Railroad run, D.W. Watts, concerning the trains and the fair, stated that: "The world's fair has brought a great increase of traffic and the railway companies have added many fast trains, trying to outdo the other and to this fact no doubt is due many of the awful wrecks...."

On October 10, 1904, the Missouri Pacific Railroad's second section No. 30 passenger train, "an exceedingly long one" had "reached Pleasant Hill, loaded with men, women and children from Southeast Kansas and Southwest Missouri, bound for the St. Louis exposition." No. 30, a "regular Missouri Pacific passenger from Joplin to Pleasant Hill," was running behind schedule and was "cut in two and the rear was attached to an engine" at Pleasant Hill, "the passenger car being immediately behind the tender with no baggage car intervening."

In the meantime, a freight train made up at Jefferson City, Mo., to Sedalia, Mo., received orders to make an added run to Pleasant Hill and keep "clear of all passenger trains." The westbound freight train was to take a siding near Montserrat and wait for eastbound 9, 10, 30, and 50 passenger trains to pass; instead, when the freight train reached Knob Noster they stopped on the siding to cool off a "hot box", so they were delayed.

After the conductor of the freight train, J.W. Preston, had made out some reports he went into the caboose and dozed off to sleep. It was reported that Conductor Preston later testified before the Coroner's jury that he had been on the job for "17 hours, had then rested 10 and that he had been at work about 12 hours when the wreck occurred." Eventually, Preston woke and in his slumber thought that he had heard the fourth passenger train go by. Preston recalled that he "went forward and asked Engineer [John D.] Horton if he was sure that all of the trains had passed. Horton replied that he was sure." Engineer Horton then gave the go ahead signal to start. Once more, for good measure, Preston inquired of Horton if he was certain, he said that he was, so they got underway – the fate of many lives was now sealed.

As the World's Fair Excursion Train No. 30 chugged onward after a brief stop at the Warrensburg depot, the dispatcher at the station being notified of the departure of the freight train at Montserrat, probably knew then and there that a "wreck was inevitable." No. 30, full to capacity with anxious passengers overflowing with anticipation of the fanfare that awaited them in St. Louis, were clueless as to what horrors loomed ahead of them only minutes down the steel rails. Valued time was running out for many of these poor, unsuspecting souls.

On a stretch of track, reportedly known as Dead Man's Curve, near Bear Creek Bridge about three miles east of Warrensburg at 3 o'clock in the wee hours of the morning, the two trains collided head-on at full speed. The Nevada *Daily* reporting on the collision stated that it was one of the "most disastrous wrecks that has happened in Missouri in recent years. Precious lives were hurried into eternity without a second warning while many persons were torn and bruised and buried beneath the debris. No words can picture the awful calamity nor describe in detail the suffering."

The first word of the disaster came to nearby Warrensburg by way of a telephone call made from a farm house that was located close to the wreck site. The awful news traveled across the countryside like a wind-blown wildfire. Available physicians and many citizens turned out to offer any assistance they could muster. The physicians were transported to the scene by special trains where they directed rescues and dressed the wounds of the injured.

TRACES OF OZARKS PAST

Newspaper reports made concerning the ordeal offered their readers information: "...the terrible shock of the collision smashed the rear passenger coaches into small fragments, killing and fatally wounding many of the occupants. Those who survived say that it is absolutely impossible to describe the agony and suffering of the injured or the condition of the dead. The passenger engines and coaches were literally sprinkled with the blood of the unfortunate and here and there upon the ragged edges of broken timbers hung pieces of clothes, flesh and blood...The scene was horrifying, the escaping steam hissed, the wounded crying for help, while the mangled and bleeding forms of the dead was enough to sicken the living."

At this point, needless to say, all the fairgoers on passenger train No. 30 had completely forgotten the happy times that awaited them in St. Louis. They would never come to pass.

The Warrensburg *Weekly Standard-Herald* made a report on October 14, four days later, saying: "The spectacle of the wreck was a sickening one. Just at dawn when the first succor arrived the sight was indeed awful. Men, women and children crazed with injuries and fright, were wandering aimlessly over the little valley calling for loved ones dead in the wreck. The dead, who were horribly mangled about the head and breast were brought out and lay beside the track. Old gray headed men and women lay beside little boys and girls, all crushed beyond recognition. The first duty of the physicians and citizens was to the wounded."

By noon, it was said that there were about five thousand onlookers lining the tracks that had assembled to view the unfolding drama. The victims of the crash were taken to an open area and laid out side by side to await a special train that would carry the "bleeding forms" back to Warrensburg.

The unthinkable catastrophe was accounted by many eyewitnesses that survived the crash. One such person, W.T. Ballagh of Nevada, Mo., recalled the awful scene: "...no one can adequately describe the horror of that awful night, the groans of the dying and cries for help of the injured, as they lay there in the debris, which was sprinkled with the dead. One instance of the pitiful crying of a little 4-year old child, begging piteously for 'mamm', was heartrending. When at last kind hands reached the child, it was dead, one of its feet touching its mother."

Laura B. Mitchell of Chetopa, Kansas, who was setting in the forward coach a couple of seats from the rear, said that: "I was seated with Mrs. W.H. Allen of Pittsburg, Kan., and had her 4 year old child in my arms...The first I knew of anything wrong I heard the air brakes begin to set and there was a rumbling sound, followed by a terrible crash and a shower of hot water, broken glass and fragments of human bodies. I kept my seat until the rush of the excited passengers was over. Everybody who was able tried to escape, but the confusion was terrible. Neither myself nor the child was seriously hurt. Mrs. Allen escaped with slight injuries. Mr. Allen and both sons were killed.

"All the lights went out as soon as the crash came and it seemed that hot steam was being blown right into our bodies. I had presence of mind enough to throw my wrap over my face and that of the little boy....

"People were killed all about me. One lady just behind me and a man just opposite me were killed. I don't see how I escaped...."

D.W. Watts was one that also survived the ordeal and as an eyewitness to it, reported that: "The air was filled [with] groans of agony, prayers and cries for help, people were crushed in a manner that was simply horrible. Not a moment's warning was given the people and we knew nothing of the freight train until we felt the terrible shock of the collision...When the wreck occurred it was not quite daylight and fires were built to give light so we could see to help those buried in the wreckage. No man can describe the scene and give any idea of the carnage and suffering. You have all read about it but have no idea how awful it was."

Another account told by W.J. Darst of Dexter, Kansas, who was also a wreck survivor, went like this: "I was seated just beyond the center of the coach next to the locomotive. We had our seats turned towards each other and were all awake and talking. I first heard the steam and the air brakes, which were being set, [and] then there was an awful crash. The lights went out. Something knocked my wife and son over, but I was not hurt, being bruised a little...I soon recovered myself and got out of the wreck. I then went to work to help get out the dead and wounded. I then found both my wife and son, who had been killed."

Hundreds of people waiting for news walked impatiently about the train station platform, strong men weeping and women sobbing. "The scene was the most pathetic ever witnessed...one that beggars description."

The victims of the crash were taken to Warrensburg and placed in the Magnolia Milling Company's grain storage building under Entertainment Hall where a coroner, Dr. Bills, impaneled a jury to identify the lost. The Nevada *Daily* offered a revised list of the dead and injured on October 11, the day after the tragedy, and listed thirty killed and fifty-four that were hurt.

As unbelievable as it may seem, there were also reports at the wreck site of the robbing of the dead. Two brakemen, E. Zeigler and L. Haynes, were arrested and jailed for "taking money from the dead bodies of the victims of the wreck." A gold pin and some money were found in the possession of the two men. Zeigler and Haynes were reported to be new to the company and had only worked for about a week. It was said that they were employed because of a shortage of men.

Among the list of the dead included passengers from the Kansas towns of: Oxford, Sedan, Coffeyville, Kingman, Edna, Dexter, Pittsburg and Cedarvale; and from Missouri: Pennsboro and Bronaugh; and there was one listed from the state of Pennsylvania. The bodies were transferred to the Minden train: four went to Bronaugh; six to Pittsburg; one to Sedan; two to Edna; and one to Dexter.

Speaking on behalf of everyone concerned, D.W. Watts was quoted in the Nevada *Daily,* saying: "...the sympathy of the entire community is extended to the relatives of those who have lost their lives and those who have been injured. It is sincerely hoped that when the details of the wreck are officially announced many of those in whom we are especially interested will be reported safe and uninjured."

The 1904 St. Louis World's Fair continued without the arrival of steam train No. 30. It went on without its human cargo of jubilant souls that were bound for the history-making exposition that

1904 St. Louis Excursion Train Disaster

celebrated the Louisiana Purchase. Instead, No. 30 seared its own place in American and Ozarks history as an ill-fated excursion ride to unspeakable tragedy.

The Warrensburg Depot located at Warrensburg, Missouri.

THE W

VOLUME XL.

FRIGHTFUL WRECK

World's Fair Excursion Crashes Into Freight at Bear Creek Bridge and Twenty-nine are Killed and More Than Sixty Injured.

What was one of the most frightful wrecks which ever occurred in the state of Missouri took place at 1:10 o'clock Monday morning just a few yards east of Bear Creek bridge, and three miles east of Warrensburg. The wrecked passenger train was what is called the second section of No. 30, and since the St. Louis exposition has been going on, has been made up at Wichita, Kansas, and run on what is called the south branch of the Missouri Pacific to Pleasant Hill where it takes the main line east to St. Louis. The freight that crashed into it was an extra made up at Jefferson City. This passenger train was an exceedingly long one when it reached Pleasant Hill, loaded with men, women and children from Southeast Kansas and Southwest Missouri, bound for the St. Louis exposition. The train was behind its schedule time, and at Pleasant Hill was cut in two and the rear was attached to an engine, the passenger car being immediately behind the tender with no baggage car intervening. When the collision

Warrensburg *Weekly Standard-Herald*, October 14, 1904.

16

1904 St. Louis Excursion Train Disaster

Bibliography

Jackson, Rex T., *1904 St. Louis World's Fair: Tragedy Along the Rails*, The Ozarks Reader Magazine, Vol. 4, No. 3, 2007.

Other Sources:

Warrensburg *Weekly Standard-Herald*, October 14, 1904.
Nevada *Daily*, October 10, 11, 12, 13, 1904.

Illustration of Mathias Splitlog from the Neosho *Times*, June 2, 1887.

Mathias Splitlog:
"Millionaire Indian" of the Ozarks

IN THE 1800s when many Native American people were relocated to the West, some to plight, poverty and uncertainty, there was one shrewd Indian, however, who faced his difficulties and made the best of it. He would go on to become a wealthy, notable man and carve out an enduring place for himself in the annals of American and Ozarks history.

Mathias Splitlog was born in 1812 in New York as a Cayuga Indian, immigrating to Ohio he met and married Eliza Barnett of the Wyandotte tribe. (Some sources say, among other things, that Splitlog was born in Canada to a Cayuga mother and a French father; and it was reported that he spoke fluent French.) But regardless of where he was born, Splitlog became part of the Wyandotte tribe and in 1843 the Splitlogs were relocated to Kansas Territory and were given status as United States citizens. He was allotted land along the rich bottom land along the Missouri and Kaw rivers in what is now Kansas City, Kansas. According to the government the Wyandotte people were "...deemed and...declared to be of the United States, and...entitled to all the rights, privileges and immunities of such citizens, and shall in all respects, be subject to the laws of the United States and the territory of Kansas, in the same manner as other citizens of said territory."

While Splitlog lived in Kansas Territory along the rivers he worked hard to eke out a living. During the American Civil War he reportedly helped patrol area waterways aboard a riverboat steamer; it was said that he had a keen knowledge and understanding of steamboat mechanics. After the war, he sold his Armourdale district property in Kansas City, Kansas for a large sum of money and became the wealthiest Native American in the world. Afterwards, Splitlog traveled to Delaware County, Oklahoma (Indian Territory) and just northeast of present-day Grove, Oklahoma, Splitlog found just what he was looking for – a clear running spring which he dubbed: Cayuga Springs. It was here, according to the Neosho *Times* dated June 2, 1887, that Splitlog "...prided himself as one clothed with all the rights of American citizenship. He has acquired large property by thrift, industry and other good qualities, and has grown to wide influence and high respectability as a border citizen resident...."

At Cayuga Springs in the Seneca Nation, in hopes of doing all he could for his people, Splitlog got busy and built a mill, school, blacksmith shop, general store, post office and a three-story factory to manufacture buggies, hacks and wagons; reportedly, coffins were also made. And west of the spring he built a hillside home. Later, in the late 1800s he would build a limestone church at Cayuga Springs as a monument to his wife; however, Eliza Splitlog died in 1894 and would not live to see its completion. Instead, two years later, its big 1,600 pound bronze Belgium-made bell tolled in honor of Eliza's life on October 25, 1896. At her death, she was the first to be buried at the cemetery located on the south side of the Cayuga Splitlog Mission named after St. Mathias. The Cayuga Splitlog Mission and Cemetery now set on a hill in Delaware County, Oklahoma overlooking the Elk River branch of Grand Lake of the Cherokees.

Not far away, just south of Goodman, Mo., in the Ozarks of McDonald County, a prospecting Frenchman, Saturna ("Doc") Benna, had purchased land there and had been searching for gold and silver. For several years Benna hoisted samples out of his mine but found only "fools gold" – iron pyrite. (The mineral is often mistaken for gold and is distinguished from the precious metal by its brittleness and hardness. Pyrite is most commonly used in the commercial production of sulfuric acid.) Eventually, a man named Moses W. Clay, an associate of Benna, devised a plan to incite a "gold rush" fever and use it to their advantage – Clay set out to gain the interest of Mathias Splitlog the millionaire Indian at nearby Cayuga Springs.

After gaining the attention of Splitlog by some, reportedly, unsavory mine "salting" of gold and other shady practices by Moses Clay, Splitlog City began to blossom under Splitlog's keen direction and abundant finances—and, in the Neosho *Times*, it had this to say: "Several months ago Mr. Splitlog became interested with M.W. Clay of this county [Newton] in a silver prospect in McDonald county and took steps to develop whatever of mineral wealth might be there hidden. They employed a mining expert of Chicago [Illinois], went to work in a business-like way, put down shafts and commenced drifting as the indications suggested. Their finds gave such encouragement that new shafts were started, additional machinery put in, all obtainable lands secured, Splitlog City laid out, a hotel and other buildings erected, and the boring of an artesian well begun to make up for the scant supply of water in that vicinity. Personally these gentlemen are reticent as to their mineral interests, though very rich specimens of silver ore have been taken from their shafts and assayed by different persons and they will not talk about selling a foot of their land beyond a mere surface right for building purposes and ordinary town business and use."

Splitlog City would soon boast of various stores, post office, blacksmith shop, printing office and newspaper (the Splitlog *Weekly News*), a 22-room hotel (the Splitlog Hotel) and other town buildings. Splitlog began to dream of a railroad through his mining town and local sentiment broadcasted its possibilities in area newspapers: "The new road is being built as an independent enterprise and while none of the large corporations have anything to do with it there is no lack of capital. Plenty of money is to be had to push it through and it is bound to be a success. A road running direct from Kansas City [Missouri] to Fort Smith [Arkansas] must as everybody can see, prove one of the best paying railroad properties in the West, and this explains why capitalists are not only willing but anxious to invest their money in it."

Before long his dream reached a milestone and on August 22, 1887, a silver spike was driven at Neosho, Mo., to commemorate the new line, the Kansas City, Fort Smith & Southern Railway. The Neosho *Times* (a weekly publication) dated August 25, 1887, recorded the historic event taking place: "...there was a noticeable stir among the people. Long before the hour appointed as the time, hundreds of people from Neosho and all parts of the country had gathered at the crossing of the Frisco and Kansas City, Ft. Smith and Southern near the fair grounds, in gleeful expectancy. About 2:30 o'clock the Splitlog and Neosho cornet bands entertained the crowd with some excellent selections of music. Mayor Bell proposed three cheers for Mathias Splitlog, and hundreds of eyes at that moment turned upon Mr. Smith, chief clerk of the Kansas City, Ft. Smith and Southern, and they were as quickly turned from him to the shining sliver-plated spike which he drew from his pocket, held it up for everybody to see and admire and then placed it in position. Mr. Splitlog raised the hammer, but the stroke was [stopped] with hammer poised above the old Indian's head, while H.O. Sittler took a photographic view of the central figure and surroundings. Three strokes sufficed to send the spike home. Then followed photographic view, after which the silver spike was withdrawn and given to Mr. Splitlog. It will doubtless be handed down from generation to another as a valued heirloom and as a souvenir of a truly notable event in American history."

Splitlog's railroad would make stops in such towns as: Neosho, Joplin, Wade, Anderson, Rutledge, Noel, and also Sulphur Springs, Arkansas. Meanwhile, newspapers echoed its benefits for the country: "In Missouri the road is chartered from Kansas City to the southern line of the State in McDonald county and in Arkansas from the northern line of that state by the most practicable route to Ft. Smith. It is almost wholly a local enterprise, with headquarters at Neosho, and embraces in its direction men of means, good judgment and plenty of pluck and energy."

Splitlog also dreamed of a line connecting Cayuga Springs to Splitlog City, but the work was abandoned, however, when he learned of the bogus "gold strike" and mine salting masterminded by his dubious partner, Moses Clay. The railroad line eventually altered its course from Splitlog City and the depot was moved to nearby Goodman.

Mathias Splitlog

Finally, in 1893, Arthur Stillwell whose grandfather was one of the founders of the New York Central and also helped construct the Erie Canal in 1825 bought the "Indian" railway and it became part of the Kansas City, Pittsburg & Gulf Railroad; it is now known as the Kansas City Southern.

About Mathias Splitlog's acceptance and treatment in Neosho, Mo. during that 19th century era, the Neosho *Times*, June 2, 1887, offered this on his behalf: "Here, as in every community, may possibly be found some narrow-minded people, whose chief passion is envy – who would build a wall around our city and refuse to let Mr. Splitlog in unless he would allow them to dictate to him all about his business, just what he should do, how and when he should do it, and all that sort of overbearing, meddlesome and selfish interference; but the mass of our citizens welcome Mr. Splitlog and enterprises to their places among us, and appreciate them for their true worth."

In 1897, while Splitlog was on a trip to Washington, D.C. for the sake of his people, he became ill and died of pneumonia. His body was returned to Cayuga Springs and he was buried next to his wife, Eliza.

Today, not much remains of that once, thriving town of Splitlog City in southwest Missouri. The mining shafts are mostly forgotten—and, for the most part, reclaimed by nature; and the town is only a dim reminder of its former glory. The same could be said of Cayuga Springs, except for the Cayuga Splitlog Mission and Cemetery perched upon the knoll with a view to Oklahoma's Grand Lake of the Cherokees. As far as Mathias Splitlog is concerned, however, many fates awaited scores of Native Americans in their own homeland after their forced removals; and even though some of Splitlog's daring enterprises did not "pan out" as he had envisioned, the story of his accomplishments and contributions are a noteworthy part of American and Ozarks history.

Cayuga Splitlog Mission built by Mathias Splitlog
—a monument to his wife Eliza.

Mathias Splitlog

Bibliography

Bradley, Larry C., *McDonald County, Missouri: A Pictorial Interpretation*, 1972.

Cook, Blanche and Cheryl, *The History of Goodman: McDonald County, Missouri*.

Jackson, Rex T., *Mathias Splitlog the "Millionaire Indian": Gold, Silver, and the "Indian" Railway*, Vol. 5, No. 3, The Ozarks Reader Magazine, Neosho, Missouri, 2008.

Rafferty, Milton D., *The Ozarks: Land and Life*, University of Oklahoma Press, 1980.

Other Sources:

Neosho *Times*, March 24, 1887.
Neosho *Times*, June 2, 1887.
Neosho *Times*, August 25, 1887.

HENRY STARR, THE NOTORIOUS OUTLAW IS SHOT HERE.

W. J. Myers, formerly of the Peoples Bank, Shoots Starr from Bank Vault While Attempting Robbery.

Headlines from the Harrison *Times*, February 19, 1921.

Outlaw Henry Starr

THROUGHOUT the vast, untamed frontier of the American West there roamed a host of gunslingers and notorious outlaws. Law enforcement, too small in number, failed to protect and serve much of the remote regions of the Wild West, especially in the Indian Nations (Oklahoma) where many desperadoes, gunfighters and infamous public enemies from all parts sought escape and refuge; they flourished, for the most part, as a result of hard times, lack of law and order, and the difficulties of the post-Civil War era.

There were gunfights and shootouts, bank holdups and train robberies, murders, hangings, jail breaks and many other events during the days of the Old West. And a great deal of it occurred in-and-around the Ozarks. One such lawless journey, however, ended in Harrison, Arkansas—a daring bank robbery that many consider marks the end of the old outlaw era.

Those lawless times brought forth many well-known figures, like Frank and Jesse James, the Youngers, Daltons, William M. "Bill" Doolin, Bartholomew "Bat" Masterson, Wyatt Earp, James Butler "Wild Bill" Hickok, Roy "Arkansas Tom" Daugherty, Belle Starr, Alf Bolin, and many, many others who did their utmost to carve out a name for themselves during those "wild and woolly" times. But eventually, the era of the gun-toting, horseback riding outlaw would at long last fade into history—it would end in the Ozarks with Henry Starr.

Henry Starr was born on December 2, 1873, near Fort Gibson in Indian Territory. Henry was born to George "Hop" and Mary Scot

TRACES OF OZARKS PAST

Starr who were part Cherokee. His grandfather was Tom Starr, an outlaw, and his uncle was the notorious Sam Starr who was Belle Starr's second husband. Belle Starr is known by many as the "Outlaw Queen" of the Old West.

When Henry Starr was only thirteen years old his father died and his mother remarried C.N. Walker—they didn't "get-along". Henry left home a few years later in 1889 and so began his run-ins with the law. While living in the Nowata area of Indian Territory he was caught with illegal whiskey. A couple of years later in 1891 he was arrested for horse theft and incarcerated in Ft. Smith, Arkansas; after jumping bail he became a wanted man. At this time, Henry Starr teamed up with some other unsavory characters and his gang robbed the Nowata Train Depot in July, 1892. A few months later in November they hit the Shufelds Store in Lenapah and the Carter Store in Sequoyah—both in the Nations. From this, for the most part, Henry Starr's life of crime and "doing time" was established.

Starr's lawless adventures came to a halt on March 27, 1915, while attempting to knock-off two banks at once—a feat the Daltons failed to do in Coffeyville, Kansas in 1892. Henry Starr and six cohorts rode into Stroud, Oklahoma and proceeded to holdup, simultaneously, the Stroud National Bank and the First National Bank. As a result, Henry and another gang member were wounded in a firefight with citizens and taken into custody; the other robbers made history and made-off with the loot. Because of this, Henry went on to spend time in the Oklahoma State Penitentiary. While imprisoned at the facility located in McAlester, Henry had a change of heart and vowed to go straight. He was paroled on March 15, 1919, for his good behavior.

Henry Starr's law abiding about-face lasted a couple of years when he became involved in Hollywood filmmaking, starring in a movie depicting the Stroud bank robbery as well as a few other films. It was during this time that he met and married his wife, Hulda, of Salisaw, Oklahoma, on February 22, 1920, and relocated to Claremore. However, the life of an outlaw was in his blood and Henry Starr's law-abiding streak came to finality about a year later.

Starr and three of his associates stole a car in Claremore belonging to a man named Rogers and headed for Harrison,

Arkansas. On February 18, 1921, the gang strolled into the Peoples National Bank of that Boone County town and according to the Harrison *Times*: "The first attempt at bank robbery in the history of Harrison was staged this morning shortly after ten o'clock at the Peoples National Bank, when Henry Starr, the notorious Oklahoma outlaw, of national ill repute, and three confederates entered the bank with drawn guns and ordered 'hands up.'"

Starr's men had the drop on the bank's cashier, Cleve Coffman, and according to the *Times*: "The affair was conducted by a master hand at this outlaw game...." However, also in the bank, ironically, was a former employee, W.J. Myers who knew where a rifle was kept in the vault, and with "coolness and courage...stepped into the vault, secured [the] rifle and fired on Starr while he was looting the open safe of its contents."

Dazed from the blast of Myers' lethal weapon and "feeling himself mortally wounded, at once saw the game was up, and ordered his confederates who were making as if to shoot Cashier Cleve Coffman, to leave without shooting anyone...." Starr may have saved Cashier Coffman's life in doing so.

When Starr's gang realized the gig was up, they fled the scene and headed for their get-a-way car which had been left on the west side of the bank. The *Times* reported that they "departed over the Crooked Creek bridge, exchanging fire with Mr. Myers, who rushed out of the bank and fired on them as they departed."

A number of armed men immediately organized a posse to pursue the bandits, but returned saying that they could only "see them fleeing in the distance." It was reported that the robbers burned their vehicle near Bellefonte (an old community of Boone County that grew up near a spring prior to the American Civil War) and disappeared into the surrounding woodlands cutting "telephone wires as they went." They eventually stole some horses to further their get-a-way—making it the last horseback robbery in American history.

Meanwhile, Henry Starr was taken to the Harrison jailhouse where physicians attended to his mortal wound. "The ball had penetrated into a vital part inflicting partial paralysis, and an incision was necessary to remove it," said the *Times*. Starr asked for chloroform and while he was undergoing treatment he requested to see Cashier Coffman to beg for his forgiveness and to find out who had shot him. When Coffman arrived Starr shook his hand and said: "You know I saved your life." The dying outlaw also wanted Coffman to remain at his side and wished for him to have his gun and that his family be "notified of his mishap." About W.J. Myers, he said: "I do not blame him at all, I would have done the same thing in his place. He was at one end of the game, and I at the other, and he won. He has a cool hand." On his lingering deathbed Starr claimed that he had "robbed more banks than any other man in the United States." He also stated that "he had never killed a man in the course of his career as an outlaw, and was glad that he had not."

Henry Starr, the nation's last Old West outlaw, died at the county jail on February 22, 1921; four days after the attempted robbery. Because of his lingering demise some of his family was present when he expired. His remains were accompanied back to Oklahoma by his "mother, Mrs. Mary Gordon, wife Mrs. Henry Starr, son Theodore Roosevelt Starr of Muskogee [Okla.], son Tonnie Starr of Homer, La., nephew Emmet Daughtery and sister Mrs. Ewing and husband." He was taken to Dewey Cemetery in Dewey, Oklahoma, and buried next to "his sister and his child [Baby Starr]"—his gravesite has no maker.

About Henry, his mother was quoted as saying the day of his death that: "Henry has always been a trial to me." "But, thank God," she went on to say, "I will know where he is tonight. I believe his character was being molded even before his birth. There was a serious uprising in Oklahoma in those days, and those dark, dangerous days must have had a prenatal influence."

The last words the dying bandit was able to speak to his mother was: "Mother, I am satisfied to die—I have made my peace with God." His final advice to his son was that he should "go straight," and "expressed regret to him for the stain placed on his name."

The bank offered a five hundred dollar reward for the arrest and conviction of the gang. The search for Starr's accomplices-in-the-crime was ongoing after he divulged their names to the authorities before he died. The gun of Henry Starr, which he gave to Cashier Cleve Coffman after the fact, is displayed in a gun collection at the

Ralph Foster Museum at College of the Ozarks in Point Lookout, Missouri. Even though some argue that the end of the Old West outlaw era might have been at a different defining moment in history, the death of Henry Starr and the horseback get-a-way of his gang after they burned and abandoned their automobile, makes the attempted bank heist at the Ozarks town of Harrison, Arkansas, a prime historical candidate of this possible distinction. While the lesson it offers, more precious than loot, continues to be a valuable one.

Bibliography

McNab, Chris, *Gunfighters: The Outlaws and Their Weapons*, Thunder Bay Press, 2005.

Young, Richard Alan and Judy Dockrey, *Outlaw Tales: Legends, Myths, and Folklore from America's Middle Border*, August House, 1992.

Other sources:

Harrison *Times*, February 19, 22, 26, 1921.

Monument to Stand Watie at the Old Ridge-Polson Cemetery located near Southwest City, Missouri.

Stand Watie:
"Red Fox" of the Confederacy

THE AMERICAN Civil War produced many capable military leaders during its five years, and a number of them became well-known and commanded troops for the North and South in the Ozarks region of Missouri, Arkansas, Kansas, and Oklahoma. For the Union there was Nathaniel Lyon, Samuel R. Curtis, James G. Blunt, John C. Fremont, James H. Lane, Frederick Salomon, and Franz Sigel; for the Confederacy there was Ben McCulloch, Sterling Price, Albert Pike, Richard M. Gano, William Cabell, Joseph O. Shelby, William Quantrill, Earl Van Dorn, and John S. Marmaduke, to name a few. One battle-hardened warrior that the War Between the States produced, having the distinction of being the only Native American to attain the rank of brigadier general for either the North or the South was Stand Watie – the "Red Fox" of the Confederacy.

Stand Watie (Degataga OO-Watee) who had a Cherokee father and a half-Cherokee mother was born near Rome, Georgia on December 12, 1806, in the old Cherokee Nation; Watie was a nephew of Major Ridge and his brother was Elias Boudinot. In favor of the Treaty of New Echota along with others of the Ridge Party, Watie relocated to the Indian Nations (Oklahoma) in 1837.

Chief John Ross (head of the Ross Party) and many of his followers were not advocates of the Cherokee Removal and the Treaty of New Echota. For this reason, the United States rounded up remaining Cherokees, about 15,000, and held them in concentration camps for their long trek westward to Indian Territory in 1838.

TRACES OF OZARKS PAST

General Winfield Scott, when gathering the last of the Cherokee resistance in the East, offered them this warning: "...troops already occupy many positions...and thousands and thousands are approaching from every quarter to render resistance and escape alike hopeless...Will you, then, by resistance compel us to resort to arms...or will you by flight seek to hide yourselves in mountains and forests and thus oblige us to hunt you down?"

Scott's men would go on to comb the precious Cherokee countryside (what the white's coveted) "with rifle and bayonet" to search "every small cabin hidden away in the coves or by the sides of mountain streams, to seize and bring in as prisoners all the occupants, however or whenever they might be found...Families at dinner were startled by the sudden gleam of bayonets in the doorway and rose up to be driven with blows and oaths along the weary miles of trails that led to the stockade."

Many perished in the detention depots from diseases and other things. When the "march" to the West finally began, they were packed into 645 wagons, "the sick, the old people, and the smaller children...the blankets, cooking pots, and other belongings [with] the rest on foot or on horses." By the time they reached Indian Territory, over 4,000 souls were lost on what became known as the "Trail of Tears" or "trail where they cried".

Stand Watie would attempt to make the most of his new life in the Nations, marrying Sarah C. Bell and having three sons and two daughters. In the northeast Indian Territory Ozarks near present-day Southwest City, Missouri, Watie would own farmland, mills, and a store. It was said of him that he was a man that spoke little but put careful thought into action, a powerful ally as well as a formidable opponent.

The feud between the Ridge and Ross Parties over the Treaty that brought them there came to a head when "Major Ridge was waylaid and shot close to the Arkansas line, his son [John Ridge] was taken from bed and cut to pieces with hatchets, while [Elias] Boudinot was treacherously killed at his home at Park Hill, Indian Territory, all three being killed upon the same day, June 22, 1839." These assassinations would leave Stand Watie the new leader of the Ridge Party.

Stand Watie

About the deadly attack on Boudinot, one report offering the gory details went like this: "The murder of Boudinot was treacherous and cruel. He was assisting some workmen in building a new house. Three men called upon him and asked for medicine. He went off with them in the direction of Wooster's, the missionary, who keeps medicine, about three hundred yards from Boudinot's. When they got about half way two of the men seized Boudinot and the other stabbed him, after which the three cut him to pieces with their knives and tomahawks. This murder taking place within two miles of the residence of John Ross...."

The new Ridge Party leader, Stand Watie, wasted no time to protect the party. He organized a company of men for revenge—and, as a result, Chief Ross and his family were forced to seek refuge at nearby Fort Gibson under the protection of the United States army.

When the Civil War broke out in 1861, Watie's sympathies were with the Confederacy. By July of 1861, Colonel Stand Watie was already recruiting and training his Cherokee Mounted Rifles at old Fort Wayne, which was located in Indian Territory just west of Maysville, Arkansas.

Fort Wayne first began on a hill overlooking the Illinois River in Adair County, Oklahoma; the hamlet of Watts inhabits the location today. On October 29, 1838, however, it was the chosen site of Camp Illinois which was later renamed Fort Wayne in honor of General "Mad" Anthony Wayne of Revolutionary War fame. The post was established by Lieutenant Colonel Richard B. Mason, 1st Dragoons, U.S. Army, in response to Arkansas citizens that feared the Indians in the neighboring territory. In 1839 the work came to a screeching halt when several soldiers became gravely ill and died, including Captain John Stuart, 7th Infantry.

In the fall of 1839, the army decided to relocate the project to what is now present-day Delaware County, Oklahoma in an area known as Beatie's Prairie, just west of Maysville, Arkansas and construct a fort there instead. Once again, the post was established by Lieut. Col. Richard B. Mason in June 1840 and dubbed Fort Wayne. The fort was to be one in a series along a road that ran from Fort Snelling, Minnesota, to Fort Towson in the southeastern part of

Indian Territory; part of it was an old Indian trace which came to be known as the "Texas Road", the "Immigrate Road to Texas", the "Fort Scott-Fort Gibson Military Road", and the "Military Road".

On May 26, 1842, the War Department chose to abandon Fort Wayne in favor of establishing Fort Scott in southeast Kansas. The log barracks and two rows of stone pillboxes that remained at Fort Wayne attracted the Confederacy early in the Civil War, which included Col. Stand Watie.

Stand Watie would become one of the most respected Civil War warriors in the Trans-Mississippi Theater, participating in many significant battles, skirmishes and actions in Missouri, Arkansas and especially Indian Territory.

Some of the first action taken during the Civil War for Col. Stand Watie and his Mounted Rifles occurred in Indian Territory, when Confederate forces of Col. Douglas Cooper under Brigadier General Albert Pike waged war on the old Creek Chief Opothleyoholo (also Hopoeithleyohola or Opothle Yahola), a loyal Unionist. Battles were fought at Round Mountain, Bird Creek, and Patriot Hills.

The largest and deadliest battle that Stand Watie participated in during the Civil War was the Battle of Pea Ridge (or Elkhorn Tavern by the South), which occurred on March 7-8, 1862, near Pea Ridge, Arkansas. Confederate Major General Earl Van Dorn's 16,000 troops of Major General Sterling Price, Brigadier General Ben McCulloch, and Brigadier General Albert Pike's Indian Force of about 1,000 including Stand Watie, faced off against Union Brigadier General Samuel R. Curtis and Brigadier General Franz Sigel's 10,500 Federals. The 2-day battle at Leetown and the Elkhorn Tavern claimed the lives of Brig. Gen. Ben McCulloch and Gen. James McIntosh of the Southern force. The loss of their commands was credited to helping turn the battle-tide in favor of the Union. According to Gen. Sigel: "The death of McCulloch was not only fatal to his troops, but also a most serious blow to Van Dorn...."

The fighting became intense in the vicinity of the Elkhorn Tavern, to which Confederate Lieutenant Colonel Walter P. Lane of the Third Texas Cavalry reported: "Silently and with stern resolve did they form for battle, and many a brave heart chafed with anxious zeal during the heavy firing which occurred near the Elkhorn Tavern."

The Battle of Pea Ridge ended when the Confederate's ammunition ran low. Col. Stand Watie's Indian force covered the Confederate retreat with a constant, heavy gunfire.

The Union charged some of Pike's Indians with tomahawking, scalping, and mutilating dead Union soldiers. Several communications between generals ensued.

Gen. Curtis ordered this message to be sent to Van Dorn on March 9, 1862: "...we find on the battle-field, contrary to civilized warfare, many of the Federal dead who were tomahawked, scalped, and their bodies shamefully mangled, and [Gen. Curtis] expresses a hope that this important struggle may not degenerate to savage warfare."

Van Dorn's Assistant Adjutant returned this reply: "...the Indians who formed part of his [Van Dorn] forces having for many years been regarded as civilized people. He will, however, most cordially unite with you in repressing the horrors of this unnatural war, and that you may co-operate with him to this end more effectually he desires me to inform you that many of our men who surrendered themselves prisoners of war were reported to him as having been murdered in cold blood by their captors, who were alleged to be Germans.

"The general commanding feels sure that you will do your part, as he will, in preventing such atrocities in future, and that the perpetrators of them will be brought to justice, whether German or Choctaw."

The use of Native Americans in the War Between the States after Pea Ridge and 1st Newtonia (Missouri) which occurred on September 30, 1862, would afterwards be confined, for the most part, to Indian Territory as a result of the tomahawking, scalping, and mutilation that were perpetrated upon the battlegrounds.

Shortly after the 1st Battle of Newtonia where the American Indian of the Blue and Gray gained the distinction of fighting against each other for the first time in the Civil War, the Battle of Fort Wayne occurred – where Native Americans would again face-off in fierce combat.

On the night of October 21, 1862, Brigadier General James G. Blunt, Commanding the First Division of the Army of the Frontier, was in hot pursuit of the Confederation of Colonel Douglas H. Cooper and Colonel Stand Watie. Gen. Blunt writes in the *Official Records of the Union and Confederate Armies* that he "left camp at Pea Ridge...with the Second and Third Brigades...consisting of the Second, Sixth, Tenth, and Eleventh Kansas and the First and Third Cherokee Regiments, the First Kansas and the Second Indiana Batteries, and four mountain howitzers, leaving the First Brigade (General Salomon) to protect [his] rear and flank and [his] supply train."

Blunt learned that Col. Cooper and Col. Watie were camped near Maysville, Ark. at old Fort Wayne with about 5,000 to 7,000 troops. He was planning an attack at daybreak but had about 30 miles to march "through a rough, wooded, and hilly country."

When Blunt reached Maysville he "stopped at a large, fine house at the edge of the prairie, and disguised as a rebel just escaped from the Federals, and wishing to get with Cooper's command" Blunt "readily enlisted the sympathies of the lady [of the house], whose husband was a soldier in the rebel camp."

After learning the strength and whereabouts of the enemy, Blunt "moved his advance across the prairie and halted a quarter of a mile from their outpost, which was at the edge of the timber, on a little wooded stream, near the town of Maysville." In the early morning hours of October 22, Blunt, hoping to keep Cooper and Watie from retreating, decided to attack with only three small companies. Blunt writes: "Advancing through an opening in the timber, about a quarter of a mile in width, I discovered the enemy in force, their line extending across the open ground in front and occupying the road."

A booming duel of cannons ensued upon the field; after which Blunt dismounted his entire regiment of the Second Kansas, advancing on the Southern position and "opening upon the rebel lines a terrific fire with their Harper's Ferry rifles." In order to take advantage of the small attacking Federal forces, Cooper counterattacked on Blunt's flanks. Fortunately for Blunt, however, the Sixth Kansas and the Third Indian Regiment "came upon the field" and advanced upon the right and the left and drove "back the flanking columns of the enemy."

The Federals then plunged into the heart of the Confederate line and captured three 6-pound brass guns, and one 12-pound brass field howitzer along with their horses, harnesses and caissons "bringing it triumph from the field." The Confederates retreated hastily to the south in disorder and did not stop until they made it to the safety of Fort Gibson; Stand Watie and his Mounted Rifles covering their retreat.

On July 2, 1863, Col. Watie suffered a terrible defeat at the 1st Battle of Cabin Creek which was fought near present-day Pensacola, Oklahoma. Watie's force attacked a supply train of Gen. James G. Blunt but without success. A few days later on July 17, 1863, the largest engagement in Indian Territory during the Civil War was waged – the Battle of Honey Springs, which came to be known by some as the "Gettysburg of Indian Territory".

About twenty miles south of Fort Gibson near present-day Rentiesville, Oklahoma, was Honey Springs – a supply depot and base of operations established by the Confederacy in the spring of 1863. Confederate General Douglas H. Cooper was at Honey Springs that summer and was hatching plans to attack and retake Fort Gibson for the Southern cause.

After Gen. Blunt had routed Col. Watie on the Military Road at 1st Cabin Creek on July 2, he continued on to Fort Gibson (also known as Cantonment Davis and Fort Blunt). Gen. Blunt had about 600 men and two artillery pieces when he arrived at the fort and learned of Cooper's nearby whereabouts and his likely reason for being at Honey Springs. He probably ascertained that Col. Watie would be there with him at the depot, as well.

More Southern troops under General William L. Cabell were also en route from Ft. Smith, Arkansas to join Cooper at Honey Springs for his play on Fort Gibson. As a result, Gen. Blunt decided to spoil their plans and attack Cooper's Confederates before Cabell could join up. Blunt, with a total of about 3,000 troops left Fort Gibson and headed for Honey Springs.

The Union forces included the 1st Kansas Colored Infantry, 1st Indian Home Guards, 2nd Indian Home Guards, 6th Kansas Cavalry,

3rd Wisconsin Cavalry, Smith's Battery, 2nd Colorado Infantry, Hopkin's Kansas Battery, and the 3rd Indian Home Guards.

Deployed along both sides of the Texas Military Road at Honey Springs, Cooper was waiting with about 5,000 Confederates consisting of the 20th Texas Cavalry, 29th Texas Cavalry, 5th Texas Partisan Rangers, Lee's Light Battery, Tandy Walker's war-painted 1st Choctaw and Chickasaw Mounted Rifles, Colonel Stand Watie's 1st and 2nd Mounted Rifles, a squadron of Texas Cavalry, and the 1st and 2nd Creek Cavalry under Colonel D.N. McIntosh.

The two combatant forces would come to blows on the north side of Elk Creek not far from Honey Springs depot. Cooper's strategic plan was to fall back on the Texas Road if it became necessary and take to the cover of the trees that grew in abundance along Elk Creek. It was reported that the Confederates were at a disadvantage because their Mexican gunpowder, for the most part, had been soaked by a summer downpour of rain and was a gooey worthless paste.

In *The American Indian as Participant in the Civil War* by Annie Abel Heloise, the author writes: "Much of the ammunition was worthless. Nevertheless, Cooper stubbornly contested every inch of ground and finally gave way only when large numbers of his Indians, knowing their guns to be absolutely useless to them, became disheartened and then demoralized."

Blunt moved his Federal troops forward until he began to draw cannon-fire from Cooper's battery. Deploying Captain Smith's big guns to the right and Captain Hopkins' guns to the left, the cannons thundered and delivered death-dealing shot, shell and canister for about an hour or more. After a continued, vigorous Federal assault on Cooper's line, the Confederacy was forced to retire to the safety of the brush and timber along Elk Creek, as planned. Blunt came within forty or fifty yards of the enemies roaring volleys while "a continuous fire was kept up for some time between the opposing lines, the colored infantry loading and firing lying down on the ground."

At one point, the armies came within twenty-five yards of each other and soon the Confederate line was "forced to retire to the south side of Elk Creek in a good deal of confusion, leaving one of their guns, which had been dismounted, and the tents and camp equipage of one regiment to fall into the hands of the Federal troops."

The Confederates tried for a spell to hold the bridge over Elk Creek as well as some fords—but, they were soon "driven from these positions by Federal infantry and the guns of Captain Hopkin's battery." Blunt's army continued their attack on Confederate forces while Cooper's rearguard cavalry units covered their retreat to the south.

Blunt discovered that Cooper's men had hastily torched the depot warehouses of supplies to keep them from being added to the Northern cause; however, one commissary building containing bacon, flour, salt and dried beef was spared and was quickly utilized by the Federals for their supper that night as they bivouacked on the Honey Springs battleground – their bellies full.

As for Gen. Cabell and his force of about two thousand men en route from Ft. Smith, Arkansas to join Cooper in the action, they were about two hours away and could hear the booming cannonade but could do nothing but join up with Cooper's troops who were licking their wounds south of the Canadian River.

For the most part, Blunt's victory at Honey Springs enabled the Union to take control of northern Indian Territory, with the exception of Stand Watie's relentless reign of terror inflicting severe damage north of the Arkansas River to Union supply bases—somehow, always eluding capture by his formidable wiles.

The bloody foray at Honey Springs that hot summer day gained several distinctions: Native Americans had again faced each other in America's Civil War; African Americans had proved their worth as fighting soldiers; the Union had gained control of the region; and the Indian Nations had hosted a significant battle that came to be known as the Gettysburg of Indian Territory.

News from Confederate President Jefferson Davis arrived to Colonel Stand Watie on May 10, 1864, while encamped at the Cherokee headquarters in the Choctaw Nation. Watie had been promoted to Brigadier General, making him the only Native American during the Civil War to achieve such a distinguished rank for either the North or the South. His loyal troops and followers broke out in celebration at the extraordinary news and marched around and around his tent to the music of the drum and fife, in honor of the "red fox" of the Confederacy.

A final military victory was added to the history books to further document the career of Brigadier General Stand Watie – the last major conflict in Indian Territory. On September 19, 1864, a 300-wagon Federal supply train on its way to Fort Gibson was camped at Cabin Creek stockade – in the same area where Watie had suffered one of his worst defeats at the 1st Battle of Cabin Creek. This time, however, Brig. Gen. Stand Watie would have his revenge.

The Union train at Cabin Creek was guarded by Captain Henry Hopkins and the 2nd Kansas Cavalry, and the 2nd and 3rd Indian Home Guard – about 600 men.

On the other hand, the Confederates under Brig. Gen. Richard Gano and Brig. Gen. Stand Watie had the 29th, 30th, and 31st Texas Cavalry, Howell's Battery, 1st and 2nd Cherokee Mounted Rifles, 1st and 2nd Creek, and a Seminole battalion – about 2,000 in all.

The Confederates began the 2nd Battle of Cabin Creek in the wee hours of the morning as "an incessant storm of shot and bursting shell swept through the camp and train, killing and wounding many of the mules, stampeding the teams, and causing inextricable entanglement in the absence of the teamsters. The bluff that rose abruptly from the creek in the rear of the camp, the stockade, and a narrow ravine on the Federal right afforded much protection to the Federal soldiers during this terrible artillery fire."

Mule teams in their panic were driven over the bluff's edge and down to the creek below. The 100 foot drop broke the wagons into pieces and killed and injured the frightened beasts of burden. Dozens of Federal soldiers died with their backs to the creek bluff, surrounded and under fire by a superior Southern force.

By 9:00 that morning, Watie's victory was complete; the Southerners gained 130 wagons loaded with commissary supplies and 740 mules—in all, a treasure trove valued at over $1,500,000. The captured supply train went a long way in the final throes of the war to help the Confederacy continue their hopeless campaign.

Finally, on June 23, 1865 (almost three months after Confederate

Stand Watie

General Robert E. Lee surrendered at Appomattox, Virginia), Brig. Gen. Stand Watie had the historical distinction of becoming the last Confederate general of the Civil War to surrender. With tears welling up in his Cherokee eyes, the old "red fox" of the Confederacy laid down his arms before Lieutenant Colonel A.C. Matthews at Doaksville, Choctaw Nation (Oklahoma) – his war was over.

Just west of Southwest City, Missouri at the old Ridge-Polson Cemetery, Stand Watie was buried on September 9, 1871. Being a Mason of high degree he received a Masonic ceremony at his funeral. On May 25, 1921, to further honor the old warrior, the Daughters of the Confederacy of Oklahoma unveiled an impressive marble stone which was added to his gravesite; it was quarried from the hills of his native Georgia homeland. A red granite monument dedicated to Stand Watie, with an engraved image of him and a useful text of signage also stands at the cemetery entrance, further testimony of his notable character and Southern service during the American Civil War.

Stand Watie's headstone at the Old Ridge-Polson Cemetery located near Southwest City, Missouri.

Stand Watie

Bibliography

Abel, Annie Heloise, *The American Indian as Participant in the Civil War*, Arthur H. Clark Company, Cleveland, 1919.

Britton, Wiley, *The Civil War on the Border*, Vol. 2, G.P. Putman's Sons, The Knickerbocker Press, New York and London, 1899; *Union and Confederate Indians in the Civil War*, Battles and Leaders of the Civil War, Vol. 1, The Century Company, 1887.

Jackson, Rex T., *Battle At Oklahoma's Old Fort Wayne: Remembering Native Americans as Veterans of the Civil War*, The Ozarks Reader Magazine, Neosho, Missouri, Vol. 4, No. 1, 2007; *At the Elkhorn Tavern: Shades of Peace and War*, The Ozarks Reader Magazine, Vol. 2, No. 1, 2005; *Gettysburg of Indian Territory: The Battle of Honey Springs*, The Ozarks Reader Magazine, Vol. 4, No. 2, 2007; *A Trail of Tears: The American Indian in the Civil War*, Heritage Books, Westminster, Maryland, 2004.

Mooney, James, *Myths of the Cherokee*, Nineteenth Annual Report of the U.S. Bureau of American Ethnology to the Secretary of the Smithsonian Institution, 1900.

Walker, Wayne T., *Soldiers in War Paint*, The West: True Stories of the Old West Magazine, March, 1967.

Illustration from the Joplin *Daily Globe*, April 16, 1903.

"Officer Down": Hate Crimes in 1903 Joplin

FROM THE LAWLESS act of a homeless man to the injustice of a bloodthirsty mob, law and order was, for the most part, ignored in the chief city of Jasper County, Missouri in the spring of 1903. Desperation seized one man while revenge, retribution and racism ignited an unstoppable firestorm of citizen violence. The historic event speaks volumes about human nature and the speed in which sound judgment can be lost to the moment. However, beneficial lessons can be gleaned from history, and the madness that gripped this Ozarks town and propelled it down this awful path those years ago, need not ever again rear its ugly head.

On April 13, 1903, the Bullock & Pierce Hardware Store in downtown Joplin, Mo., was robbed. The proprietor, Sam Bullock, reported to the authorities that two pistols had been taken from the store. In response to the robbery, according to the Joplin *Daily Globe* dated April 15, Police Officer Theodore Leslie decided to make a search in the Kansas City Southern train yard for "...some tramps and when he reached the end of a string of box cars which were standing on the siding, a negro was seen standing on the east side of the car." While Officer Leslie was searching the man, Charles O'Brien, shots rang out from inside a boxcar. Leslie emptied his gun in a blazing firefight, but as he was firing his last shot "...a bullet from his antagonist's gun pierced his right eye and he fell to the ground and expired almost instantly." The outlaw inside the train car was seen jumping from it, heading north. O'Brien was taken into custody for further questioning while the body of Officer Leslie was taken to the city morgue for examination—it was learned that Leslie had been hit by a second bullet which had pierced his chest.

About the officer's time spent on the Joplin police force, the *Daily Globe* offered this: "Officer Leslie was placed on the force one year ago this month and he proved a most efficient officer. He knew no fear and was always to be found at his post, and covered one of the most difficult beats in the city, being from Second street north. He was about 36 years of age and leaves a wife and four children...."

A number of gathered citizens gave chase to the boxcar shooter and more shots were fired, but as it was growing dark they were forced to abandon their pursuit. A search of the train car revealed evidence that could probably link the suspect to area crime. As word spread like wildfire people poured-in from all corners to demand justice.

The next day, April 15, according to the Joplin *Daily News Herald*, "A posse of a dozen armed men found the negro [the alleged shooter] hiding beneath a pavilion in Midway park. From the fact that he had a gun shot wound in his left leg, the members of the posse were confident that they had captured the murderer of the policeman." However, the *Daily Globe* reported that the capture was made by Lee Fullerton and M.R. Bullock at a slaughter house near Midway Park. The suspect was Thomas Gilyard, a 20-year-old African American man.

Gilyard, as of yet innocent until proven guilty, was taken to the city jail where he was placed in an inner cell. The news of his capture was music-to-their-ears as the waiting, angry public had begun to gather in large numbers—an assault on the east side door began at once. The *Daily News Herald* gave the details: "Two dozen men secured a heavy piece of timber and by continuous battering the frail door gave away and the mob rushed inside...the cell was broken open and from a dark corner of the place in which the negro was crouching the man was dragged forth by main force. His leg was so badly injured that it was impossible for him to walk. The mob went wild with excitement and thousands of people crowded the thoroughfares and thronged on the housetops as the negro was dragged through the dust to his doom."

The hate-mob couldn't get enough to satisfy their lust as they grew louder with their "awful concourse which demanded the prisoner's life. The crowd was by this time swelled to thousands. Like a terrible vortex of raging billows the mob swayed and struggled and fought to reach the object of its wrath."

The treatment of Gilyard was savage and inhuman. The *Daily Globe* informed its reader that "...he was beat and cuffed and trampled and choked, until...he was almost dead."

Thomas Gilyard was taken to the corner of Second and Wall to the sounds of men, women and children screaming out such things as: "Get a rope!" "Hang the negro!" "Hang the murderer!" "Kill him!" and "Lynch the nigger!"

While all of this was playing out, some officials, Dr. F.E. Rohan, Perl Decker, Mayor Cunningham and other concerned citizens begged the bloodthirsty crowd to let law and order take its rightful course—their wise words were ignored. It was like a "tug of war" between the lawful minded and the lawless, but in the end the almost nude body of Gilyard was won by the latter. After a rope was placed over a telephone pole and secured around Gilyard's neck he "was hoisted from the ground...As the body slowly ascended the negro's tongue lolled from his head and his face was contorted in awful agony." The condemned man's pleas of innocence had fallen on deaf ears, and "one lone shot was fired at his dangling body" and the dirty deed was done.

Two years before on April 23, 1901, two other Joplin police officers, Bert Brannon and Charles Sweeney, were also killed in the discharge of their duty by a gang of vagrants—the killers were never apprehended for the crimes. This undoubtedly weighed upon the public.

After the lawless lynching, it didn't stop there, bands of irate people marched down Main Street yelling "Down with the negroes" and "Hang the coons." Many racial threats were leveled at Joplin's innocent African American population. "At the corner of Fifth and Main streets the mob, now grown larger and more frenzical, declared that every negro must leave the city by tomorrow morning."

The streets again filled with an "inflamed horde" bent on revenge and fueled by pent up racism. "Every means was exhausted by the police...to stay the carnage" but the fever-pitch was too high to calm.

The first attack occurred on the northern edge of Main Street where a "half dozen negro shanties were set on fire." Their wrath was relentless as the mob hurled "rocks and missiles of all descriptions...at the houses, through windows and at fleeing negroes." The local fire department amidst "taunts and jeers" did their utmost, however, to extinguish the roaring fires. "As fast as a line of hose was strung the mob stuck knives into it."

After this, over a thousand strong ascended upon the eastern part of the city and resumed their hate-crimes; as well as torching more homes on East Seventh Street. Needless-to-say, the actions drove out many African Americans from Joplin.

About their hasty exodus, the *Globe* had this to say: "Negro women carrying bundles of clothes tied in bed sheets, baskets and grips were to be seen in all directions...all day. They were leaving the city and every car that left Joplin was loaded with them...Many of the negroes sold their furniture in order to get money enough to purchase tickets out of town...."

"The houses burned by the mob...were residences of some of the best negroes in the city, and the action of that mob has been condemned by the law-abiding citizens of Joplin."

Headlines in the Joplin *Daily News Herald*, April 17, 1903, warned: "Five Hundred Citizens With Guns Preserve Joplin's Name From Further Stain or Blemish."

Finally, after all the violence and burning had subsided, about 500 good citizens of Joplin responded to the mayor's call-to-arms and Colonel Joel T. Livingston was made grand marshal. The armed citizens "had a magic effect on the multitude. In five minutes the streets were cleared and those who had prepared for a night of rioting were doomed to disappointment. Men moved away in every direction...Every time there was an evidence of a gathering the armed citizens quickly dispersed it.

"Officer Down"

"Crowds from Carthage, Webb City and Galena [Kansas] poured in on every car. There were a few 'bad' men from Pierce City it is said, but the delegation, which rumor had it, was coming from that place, did not arrive."

The headline of the April 17 addition of the Joplin *Daily Globe* read: "Leaders of the Mob Will Be Prosecuted." After hearing the evidence, the names Sam Mitchell, Barnes, and "Hickory Bill" Fields were implicated as the mob leaders during the lynching of Thomas Gilyard. However, no warrants were issued against Barnes and Mitchell, but Fields was eventually charged with arson over the burning of some of the homes during the riot.

The unfortunate incident has left its mark deep into the tracks and traces of Joplin's colorful history; and civilized society still, at times, wrestles with hate crimes and all forms of lawlessness. But history teaches us to look back and learn, and see for ourselves what we might strive to overcome in building a better future.

Bibliography

Jackson, Rex T., *"Officer Down": 1903 Hate Crimes in Southwest Missouri*, The Ozarks Reader Magazine, Vol. 7, No. 3, 2010.

Other Sources:

The Joplin *Daily Globe*, April 15, 16, 17, 1903.
The Joplin *Daily News Herald*, April 15, 16, 17, 1903.

Illustration of Officer Theodore Leslie
from the Joplin *Daily Globe*, April 15, 1903.

The Oak Lawn Cemetery in West Plains, Missouri, and the monument to many of the victims. (Photo by the author.)

Dancing Into Eternity: Disaster at the Old Shrine Hall

A JUBILANT GROUP of souls unaware of a shocking, unforgiving catastrophe about to unfold were undoubtedly enjoying themselves on a spring night in the Ozarks. The orchestra music carried them gracefully around the dance hall floor and swept them to realms of joy and contentment—but, the "grim reaper" had other plans for them. A tremendous explosion would send 37 people into eternity, leaving friends, loved ones, family members and a grief-stricken community in awe of the devastation and loss.

On April 13, 1928, the peaceful town of West Plains, Missouri, was rocked by disaster at 11:05 p.m. About sixty people were attending a dance at the Bond Dance Hall (old Shrine Hall), along with musicians, when a powerful explosion occurred. The dance hall was located on the second floor of a building on East Main Street, but the blast originated on the first floor which was occupied by the Wiser Motor Company. The explosion was heard 26 miles away in Mountain View to the north, as well as in many other places.

The Howell County *Gazette* headlines read: "37 Dead, 22 Hurt, In Fatal Explosion," while the West Plains *Weekly Quill* cried: "37 Killed in Mystery Blast; 22 Injured."

There were a couple of explosions: the first was said to have been a light one, but the second one sounded like a bomb had been detonated which left the whole block in flames; the ground trembled and the dance-goers were engulfed in life-taking fire and debris. It was reported that the dance floor rose up from the force of the explosion "like the deck of a ship in a storm."

The sounds of trapped victims in piteous agony could be heard in the flaming rubble of what remained of the Bond Dance Hall and Wiser Garage. Citizens that first responded on the scene witnessed injured and bleeding souls crawling out of the fire-trap—they did their best to help rescue them. Eventually the fire department arrived and kept a constant stream of water "on the smoking ruins of the dance hall."

The catastrophe devastated and damaged several other buildings including the West Plains Bank and Howell County Courthouse, as well as blowing out windows two blocks away. When the fire was finally under control, the gruesome task of recovering bodies began. By this time the scene was further saddened by the arrival of family and friends of the lost with their tears and screams as familiar and unfamiliar bodies were displayed one-after-the-other. Many of the fire victims were burned beyond recognition and would never be identified. The first victim to be recovered from the ruins was Paul Evans, Jr., and soon after, Mrs. Robert G. Martin's body was found. The injured survivors were quickly transported to the Christa Hogan Hospital.

Speculation as to the cause of the explosion and consuming fire may have gone to the grave with J.W. "Babe" Wiser, owner of Wiser Motor Company who was also a victim of the tragedy. No one could ascertain as to whether or not it was an accident or deliberate. The coroner's verdict of April 23, 1928, concluded that the "fire and explosion is unknown to [the] jury." Though there were other theories, the most common was that the explosion was caused by gasoline in the garage below.

Reporters and photographers came from near and far to cover the event. In time, however, thousands of people turned out to view "ground zero" and watch workers mining through the mangled mess for any other bodies or clues yet to be recovered or discovered.

Twenty of the unidentified victims of the Bond Dance Hall tragedy were laid to rest in silver-gray caskets and buried together in two rows in unmarked graves at the Oak Lawn Cemetery in West

Plains—a few blocks east and south of the downtown square. Thousands attended the funeral with bowed heads and broken hearts. "It was the most pathetic scene ever witnessed in West Plains."

A large granite "Rock of Ages" monument with the names of the twenty was finally erected on the site on October 6, 1929. The names are as follows: Miss Mary Adair, Miss Frances Drago, Mrs. Wallace Rogers, Robert Murphy, Mrs. Robert Murphy, Miss Ruth Fisher, Marvin Hill, Evelyn Conkin, Esco Riley, Mrs. Esco Riley, Miss Icy Risner, Boyd Garner, Carson McClelland, Chester Holstein, Miss Beatrice Barker, Miss Juanita Laws, Miss Ruby Hodkinson, Newt Riley, James Loving, and Hugh Sams.

The names of the identified dead are: R.G. Martin, Mrs. R.G. Martin, Kitty McFarland, Mrs. Carl Mullins, Paul Evans, Jr., Chas. Fisher, Major Bob Mullins, J.W. Wiser, John Bates, Charles Merk, Julian C. Jeffery, Carl Jackson, Miss Dimple Martin, Lev Reed, Hazel Slusser, Ben Jolly, and Clinton Clemmons.

Some of the victims were prominent figures in the community, such as Mrs. Sula Gaines Martin who was the daughter of Confederate Colonel R.G. Maxey. Mrs. Martin was also a leader of the Daughters of the American Revolution, Order Eastern Star, Daughters of the Confederacy, Woman's Business Club and vice chairman of the Democratic committee of Howell County. Mr. and Mrs. Martin were buried at the Elmwood Cemetery in Memphis, Tennessee; their beautiful daughter, Miss Dimple Martin, who played the piano in the orchestra that fateful night, was also buried at Elmwood Cemetery in Memphis. Young Dimple had, a couple of years earlier, won a movie tryout at the Newman Theater in Kansas City, Mo., in a beauty contest. She had also participated in a number of local talent shows and programs. The song being played at the time of the blast was—ironically, *At Sundown.*

One man that survived the burning of one of the buildings on the block, the Adams Building, was Frank K. Poole who was a Union veteran of the American Civil War. Apparently he must have had "9 lives" since he had lived through the bloody Civil War and had escaped the horrible fire, as well.

The number of people affected by this disaster was many, and it took years for things to return to some sort of normalcy. The town, at times, was called the "City of the Dead". Today, the horror of that eventful night still lingers in the conscience of the West Plains community. But even though the beautiful music and lively dance floor changed in that terrible moment, sweet memories of those lost souls who danced into eternity are ever present.

Bibliography

Jackson, Rex T., *Dancing Into Eternity: Disaster at the Bond Dance Hall*, The Ozarks Reader Magazine, Vol. 7, No. 2, 2010.

Other Sources:

Howard County *Gazette*, April 19, 1928
West Plains *Weekly Quill*, April 19, 1928

Y, JANUARY 18, 1917.

FAIRVIEW BANK ROBBED.

Three Men From Automobile Hold Up Cashier and Take Nearly $5,000.

About three o'clock Monday afternoon a big automobile drove up to the First National Bank at Fairview, 17 miles east of Neosho. Three men got out and went into the bank while one man stayed at the wheel. Inside the bank the three men presented revolvers and made Cashier Geo. Swindle and his wife and the bookkeeper, G. C. Nichols, hold up

Headlines from the Neosho *Times*, January 18, 1917.

1917 Newton County Bank Robbery

BACK IN THE early part of the 20th century, especially during the Depression and Prohibition era of the Roaring Twenties and Thirties, lawlessness abounded. During that time there were criminals and gangsters roaming the countryside looking for their next victims to plunder, such as Bonnie and Clyde (Barrow Gang), Barkers and Karpis Gang, "Machine Gun" Kelly, Dillinger, "Pretty Boy" Floyd and many others. Those unique, hard times also spawned a multitude of small-time outlaws that dreamed of an easier life with food in their bellies and money in their pockets. However, many of these outlaws learned the hard way that crime does not pay. An armed robbery in Newton County, Missouri offered just such an occasion.

One winter afternoon on January 15, 1917, the First National Bank of Fairview was suddenly and without warning facing three masked men brandishing revolvers and demanding money. While a fourth man waited outside in a get-a-way car with the motor running (reportedly a new six cylinder Buick), the three robbers inside the bank ordered Cashier George Swindle, his wife and a bank bookkeeper, according to the Neosho *Times*, to "hold up their hands and face the wall...." The officials were helpless and being robbed at gunpoint!

The Neosho *Daily Democrat* reported that "The robbers pointed revolvers at the bank officials and after making the cashier open the safe they marched all three into the vault...." However, the banker's wife had the presence of mind to hold the "...combination of the lock on the inside and kept the door from locking."

Meanwhile, the thieves, according to the *Democrat*, "...treated the bank officials courteously and took their time in looking for money, securing every cent in the bank, even the pennies." The desperadoes managed to grab up about $4,000 in cash before returning to their motorized accomplice waiting outside. They quickly made their escape and "turned their machine and drove west to the first corner and then turned north, going at a very rapid speed."

Back in the bank, the cool head of Mrs. Swindle enabled them to easily let themselves out of the vault. The *Times* bragging about how she had "outwitted the robbers," added this: "...as soon as the robbers were outside the three bank officials came out and gave the alarm."

Witnesses standing across the street from the bank also responded. The *Times* wrote that the witnesses saw the crooks "...go into the bank and that some remarks were made in a jocular way about the bank being robbed. As soon as the automobile had passed them they went over to the bank and found out the truth. The alarm was given and telephone messages were sent to all surrounding towns."

Soon after the holdup, Constable Hodges of Fairview organized a posse to hunt down the outlaws chasing after them in a Ford, but before long their vehicle reportedly developed some "tire trouble" and they lost valuable time. However, the bandits were "...traced north to Wentworth and were heard of near Reeds but the trail was lost about dark."

Other nearby law officers, such as Neosho's Sheriff Sanders, Deputy Mayfield and H.S. Bales eventually joined the manhunt. And there were several sightings and reports from area citizens about seeing the speeding get-away car. One report in the *Democrat* stated that: "It bore no number but had a tag bearing the words 'License Applied For.'" Some believed that they had probably made it to Webb City or Joplin and that if they abandoned their car there, it would be very difficult if not impossible to find them.

1917 Newton County Bank Robbery

It took about a month to finally track down the perpetrators of the daring crime; they were Albert Johnson, Willard Massey, Jesse Cutler, and the infamous outlaw Roy "Arkansas Tom" Daugherty. The Neosho *Times* had this to say about the historic event: "It is probably the most successful bank robbery that ever took place in this county."

The First National Bank of Fairview opened on December 11, 1908, and closed because of the effects of the Depression on September 16, 1930. As it turned out, the hard times of that era not only, undoubtedly, prompted the lawless raid on the bank, but, ironically, also victimized the bank yet again when it finally caused its demise thirteen years later.

Bibliography

Jackson, Rex T., *The First National Bank of Fairview: Robbery, Victim of Hard Times*, The Ozarks Reader, Vol. 6, No. 1, 2009.

Other Sources:

Neosho *Daily Democrat*, January 16, 17, 1917.
Neosho *Times*, January 18, 1917.

Monument and plaque in Hurley, Missouri.

Civil War Bushwhackers in Stone County

HERE IN THE OZARKS the American Civil War caused scores to live in fear and uncertainty. Regular army troops, guerrillas and bushwhackers came near to or visited almost every household. This was the case of one unsuspecting family that lived in Stone County, Missouri, on a hot, dark August night in 1861.

On the south edge of Hurley, Mo., curious souls interested in the struggles of the 19th century and how those adversities were sometimes dealt with, can find a small commemorative stone and plaque dedicated to John and Lydia Short by their descendants. It reads: "On this spot during the Civil War, two Confederate soldiers attacked John Short, a Union man. Lydia Coleman Short, John's wife, killed one Confederate with an ax during the savage struggle. The other escaped."

The town of Hurley was located near the historic Old Wire Road (used extensively by the military at that time) and where the Butterfield Overland Mail Route ran before the outbreak of the Civil War. The trace was a trail of trouble for many that lived on or near it, but it was here in this scenic Ozarks valley where John and Lydia made their home.

Relocating to the northern part of Stone County from Tennessee, the Shorts made the best of it on their Missouri farm. When the War Between the States broke out, however, John voiced his support for the Union and offered his services to General Nathaniel Lyon who was in Springfield, Mo., in the summer of 1861. As a result, John would become a guide and scout for the Union army.

Also in the area at that time was Confederate General Sterling Price and a large Southern force. On August 2, 1861, just south of where the bloody Battle of Wilson's Creek was waged a few days later on the 10th, General Lyon engaged Price's advance guard at a place known as Dug Springs. Union Captain Frederick Steele, Second U.S. Infantry, writing about the Skirmish of Dug Springs, describes in the *Official Records of the Union and Confederate Armies* the ruff and rugged Ozarks terrain: "From our position the valley sloped towards that of the enemy up to the foot of the hill, where it turned off to their right. From behind the hills, on our left, was a deep ravine, running towards the enemy's position. The bed of a dry stream ran along to the left of the road, and in places was deep, and skirted with tall, thick brush-wood...In a country of such conformation it was impossible for us to form any estimate of the enemy's strength." It was helpful, under these circumstances, to know the area, and for this reason military guides and scouts that were familiar with the landscape, like John Short, were utilized.

About that summer clash at Dug Springs, William M. Wherry who wrote the article *Wilson's Creek, and the Death of Lyon* which appears in one of the volumes of *Battles and Leaders of the Civil War* published in 1887, reported that: "During those blistering August days the men marched with bleeding feet and parched lips, Lyon himself urging forward the weary and footsore stragglers."

After the action at Dug Springs, and since the skirmish was only a few miles distance from John Short's farm, he asked to be granted a leave of absence to return home. No one knows whether or not he was followed, or whether the proximity of the Short farm to the Old Wire Road, his Northern sympathies or some other twist of fate spawned the following tale to unfold, but the bizarre event is now documented for all times in Ozarks history.

John arrived home without a "hitch", had supper and settled down to relax for the rest of the evening before "turning in". Suddenly, two men showed up and inquired about the location of the Springfield Road—they claimed they wanted to reach the Union army. Wanting to be helpful, John strolled out to the fence in the front yard and bolted over it to continue conversing with the strangers; or possibly he might have gone out there to keep them further from the house, thinking of his wife. "No sooner had he struck the ground than a pair of stalwart arms were thrown around him, pinning his arms to his sides," according to *The Ozarks Region: Its History and Its People*.

Short went down to his knees while he attempted to draw his pistol, "...with one ruffian choking him and the other grappling for the pistol, on which the attacked man still managed to keep his grip. But the odds were too great; Short felt his strength going fast and knew that he could hold out but a moment longer."

All at once he felt their hold on him slacken. One of his attackers quickly fell to the ground while the other one scampered pell-mell down the road. "In an instant Short was on his feet, his revolver cracked and the fleeing man leaped into the air and came down with a bullet through his heart."

Still not knowing what had happened to the second one, Short turned back and was amazed to see him lying "flat on his face, and under his shoulder blade Short's axe was sunk almost out of sight!"

Apparently, a brave, frightened, loving Lydia Short had gone to the woodpile, retrieved the ax and "with one swift, sure stroke, had slain the man who was choking her husband to death." It was kill or be killed, she believed.

During the fight Lydia had overheard the attackers saying that some of their comrades could "arrive at any moment," and fearing for her beloved husband, "she insisted that he take his gun and blanket, and spend the night in the woods." At first, John resisted thinking that her safety was equally important; however, he finally relented and left Lydia "alone with those dead scamps."

Lydia chose not to light any lamps for fear of attracting more trouble, but instead spent her time dragging the dead bodies behind the house where she dug a shallow grave and "rolled them in, and covered them up." Furthermore, she added a pile of straw over the grave to hide her handiwork, even more.

Sure enough, in the morning about 30 men arrived and asked whether she had seen the two men. She told them she had not seen them. They also wanted to know about her husband, but she told them he was away in Springfield. Afterwards, the "gang of thieves ransacked the house, taking everything that struck their fancy, while the brave woman sat in her chair and freely told them her opinion of men who would rob a helpless woman."

Before they left, however, they attempted to set fire to their "feather bed, and threw a shovel full of coals from the fire place into the straw underneath the bed. That was the way many a home was burned in those days." Like a flash "Mrs. Short sprang to her feet, gathered the blazing straw tick in her arms, and cast it over the front fence." The house was saved.

The horrific events of that dark night reveal an era when terror and lawlessness blossomed, and safety and security was elusive and uncertain. It also shows to what extent love, selflessness, and self-preservation can compel someone confronted by such dire trials and tribulations.

In 1962 a plaque was erected in honor of John and Lydia Short; and to document that historic night. According to the signage, however, one of the bushwhackers escaped—a difference in the account recorded in *The Ozarks Region: Its History and Its People*; that account was given to the author of that book about 10 years after the incident. It is also believed that the bushwhackers are still buried there to this day, along that old trail.

Bibliography

Jackson, Rex T., *Civil War Times: Bushwhackers in Stone County*, The Ozarks Reader Magazine, Vol. 6, No. 3, 2009. Springfield, Missouri: Interstate Historical Society, *The Ozarks Region: Its History and Its People*, Volume 2, 1917.

Ernest and Eula Jackson at Kel-Lake Motel.

Kel-Lake Motel:
An Icon of Route 66

OF ALL the traces that have traversed the Ozarks and beyond, one is remembered above the rest—Route 66. Along this well-traveled American road many businesses took advantage of the heavy traffic, set up shop and became successful. For many weary travelers after a long day at the steering-wheel, the need for sleep became overwhelming and the neon motel signs prompted them to pull over and abandon their beloved machines. Kel-Lake Motel was one of those old Route 66 icons that attracted its share of slumbering customers. Located just east of Carthage, Missouri across from Kellogg Lake, this overnight stop will forever embrace the history that spotlights Route 66.

Since ancient times, roads have been important and have helped to further civilization; and being able to easily travel from one place to another has always been a challenge to overcome. During the Roman Empire, for example, about 50,000 miles of ancient Roman road was constructed, and some of it still remains. The first American colonies, however, used the rivers as highways but eventually established trails along the Atlantic seacoast by the coming of the Revolution; and many more roads followed.

By the 19th century, brick and sheet asphalt were being tried to pave city streets, as the need for better roads increased with the advent of bicycles and horseless carriages (automobiles). During this era, plank and corduroy roads were also constructed which were made of rough wooden planks or logs. However, the eight to 12-feet wide roads were abandoned for a number of obvious reasons—freezing and thawing as well as warping and decay. One of the most well-known wooden roads in the Missouri Ozarks was the Ste. Genevieve, Iron Mountain, Pilot Knob Plank Road. It meandered about 42 miles from Ste. Genevieve through Farmington to Iron Mountain, and was completed by 1853.

Route 66 is by far the most famous of all roads and was commissioned on November 11, 1926, in Springfield, Mo., in the Woodruff Building located on St. Louis Street. The new highway was approved by the Federal Interstate Highway System in Springfield because of its location as the "crossroads of America", being at the intersection of Highways 65 and 66; it also made Springfield the "birthplace of Route 66". This important, historic trace became known as "The Main Street of America", "The Way West", "The Mother Road", "The Will Rogers Highway" and "The Road of Dreams".

"66" originally ran 2,448 miles from Chicago, Illinois, to Los Angeles, California and the Pacific Ocean at Santa Monica; Santa Monica was, finally, officially designated as the Western Terminus of Route 66 on November 11, 2009. Along this historic route many unique and interesting businesses were established to cater to the wayward traveler in search of the spirit that haunted this magical highway. In many cases, flashing neon lights or huge billboards beckoned to the curious or weary road warriors to stop and enjoy—and so they did! There were cafés, motels, historic sights, unique and one-of-a-kind attractions, scenic overlooks and much, much more.

The blacktop ribbon sliced through the Missouri Ozarks from St. Louis to Joplin, and its roadside delights were many. One of those old Route 66 icons was Kel-Lake Motel. "Kel-Lake" was owned by Ernest and Eula Jackson during part of the Mother Road's heyday from about 1955 to 1965; this was before the completion of Interstate I-44.

During the years that the Jackson's owned and operated the motel, many people cruising along the highway from all parts took notice of the neon vacancy sign and rented rooms for $5 to $7 per night. They were treated to clean overnight accommodations and full-size beds, air conditioning and more.

On one occasion the eight-room motel was visited by major league baseball player, Johnny Callison, of the Philadelphia Phillies; it was the same year he played outfield in the All-Star game and hit a home run. There were other famous people that stayed at Kel-Lake as well, such as President Harry S. Truman's sister who was in town attending an event. And there were people from all over America and many foreign countries that "checked" into this historic icon during those years.

Hitchhikers and hobos also visited Kel-Lake Motel. Ernest, seeing their needs, would often give them sandwiches and offer them a place to sleep in his 1953 Chrysler that was kept out front to help give the appearance that there were always visitors—even during slow times, which was seldom the case on busy Route 66. And anglers that fished the waters of Kellogg Lake across the highway would come over to catch the "tobacco spitting" grasshoppers that liked to cling to the red brick of the motel, which they used for bait.

The heavy traffic was also the cause of a number of terrible car and truck crashes at the dangerous intersection where Kel-Lake Motel was located. Ernest was often the first responder to offer assistance while Eula was calling the authorities—ambulance and police. Once, while he was making preparations to free a man pinned in a car, a highway patrolman arrived on the scene and decided it was best not to make the attempt. As a result, the poor injured motorist died before the ambulance arrived. In those days there were no paramedics or en route lifesaving procedures; instead, ambulances (usually Cadillac station wagons) relied on a high-rate-of-speed to save lives.

When "check out" time came, Ernest's first order of business was to inspect rooms in case visitors might have stolen motel property. On one occasion, after the inspection of a certain room, Ernest discovered missing towels, a television set and other things; however, instead of calling the sheriff he headed east on Route 66 in his high-powered 1959 Buick and pulled over the thief and retrieved the lost items.

TRACES OF OZARKS PAST

A visit to Kel-Lake Motel would not have been as memorable without knowing its primary hosts. Ernest and Eula were born in 1922 and were raised in northwest Missouri. They farmed near Hopkins, Mo., and eventually relocated to southwest Missouri buying the newly constructed Kel-Lake Motel in the mid-1950s. Ernest was a very patient man when it came to his work and didn't believe in throwing anything away; he would spend hours fixing something that others would quickly throw away—he didn't believe in waste. He enjoyed nature, farming, livestock, travel, common sense, making "ends meet", his four children and a host of other things. Ernest died September 24, 1998, and is buried on a hill overlooking Hopkins along with other family members. His years spent at Kel-Lake Motel during the heyday of Route 66, and his many contributions to its significance in American history, has forever linked him to that special period in time.

Truly, Route 66 delivered many the opportunity of a lifetime to experience America and get to know some of its citizens, like Kel-Lake Motel's Ernest Jackson. Today, the old historic trace can still give a glimpse into that same spirit that once reached out and touched so many travelers on America's Main Street—history's most famous stretch of road.

Kel-Lake Motel

Above: Kel-Lake Motel's first postcard. Below: The motel's second postcard.

Author's illustration of Bill Doolin.

"Oklahombres" Chieftain Bill Doolin

OF THE MANY footprints left behind in the hills and vales of Ozarks history, the outlaws of the Old West have left their share. A large majority of these 19th century desperados that made enduring names for themselves, "holed up" in Indian Territory (Oklahoma); and sometimes their handiwork would spill over into neighboring states.

The lawlessness that existed in the Nations was a magnet for this sort of rough and rugged character, and many of them would eventually rob trains, stagecoaches and banks. However, in the process of executing these criminal acts they did even worse—they committed murder. As a result, they became wanted by the law and were forced to live life on the run to avoid being captured. Many of them were hunted down, shot in battle, incarcerated, or faced the noose for their many crimes. Their names are noted in the annals of history as lessons to the future; one such outlaw is the infamous Bill Doolin.

William M. "Bill" Doolin was born in 1858 in Johnson County, Arkansas, to Michael and Artemina Doolin, who were farmers. When Bill was 23-years-old he decided it was "high" time to leave his Ozarks "nest" and head west to Indian Territory. Before long, he found employment as a cowhand at the H-X Bar Ranch (some sources say the Turkey Track Ranch), which was located northwest of Guthrie in present-day Logan County. Things went well until

1891 when Doolin was involved in a shooting at Coffeyville, Kansas. As the story goes, a couple of deputy sheriffs raided a cowboy beer party which included Bill Doolin, and during the affair the lawmen poured the "brew" out on the floor and Doolin and the drunken rancheros gunned them down over it.

After participating in the beer party shoot-out, and after having made the acquaintance in that area with several members of the large Dalton family—Grattan (Grat), Robert (Bob), Emmett, and William (Bill), Doolin joined the Dalton gang. As a result, Bill Doolin's historic life of crime was established. He would go on to become an outlaw icon of the American West.

For several months the Doolin-Dalton gang robbed a number of trains and railroad depots, but for some reason Doolin did not accompany the gang when it decided to attempt a history-making two-bank heist at Coffeyville, Kan., on October 5, 1892; some sources claim that Doolin's horse turned up lame which prevented his participation in the Coffeyville raid; while others contend that Doolin and Bill Dalton argued with the rest of the gang that the robberies were too risky and they refused to go along with the plan. Regardless of the reason for Doolin and Bill Dalton not attending the robbery attempt, it was a good choice on their part since Emmett Dalton was the only raider to survive it.

Bob, Grat, Emmett, Bill Powers and Dick Broadwell rode into Coffeyville about 9:40 a.m. Grat, Broadwell and Powers would enter the Condon Bank and Bob and Emmett the First National Bank. While they were inside the banks, a citizen who had recognized them alarmed other townspeople who quickly made ready to receive them when they came out. A blazing gun battle occurred as the outlaws attempted to make their daring getaway with their bags of money. Several of the town's "defenders" perished along with most of the Dalton gang. Soon after, Bill Doolin would take over as chieftain of the notorious gang.

Doolin would organize his famous "Oklahombres" enlisting a host of notorious gang members, such as Bill Dalton, "Red Buck" Weightman, Dan "Dynamite Dick" Clifton, "Little" Dick West, Roy "Arkansas Tom" Daugherty, "Little" Bill Raidler, William "Tulsa Jack" Blake, George "Bitter Creek" Newcomb, Alf Sohn, Bob

Bill Doolin

Grounds, Charley Pierce and Ole Yantis.

Ironically, in 1893, a few months after the Coffeyville raid by the Daltons, Doolin found the time in his busy criminal life to "tie-the-knot" with the daughter of a Christian minister who lived near present-day Quay in Payne County, Oklahoma. Doolin's wife, Edith, would eventually give birth to a son.

On September 1, 1893, the Doolin gang was attacked in the outlaw town of Ingalls, Oklahoma, by a posse of lawmen in Trojan Horse-type covered wagons. Not long after the wagons full of officers entered the town, a great battle ensued which is second only to the historic western gunfight at the OK Corral. By the time the black powder smoke had cleared, the Doolin gang had made their escape. The only exception was Arkansas Tom who was captured; he had covered his comrades' retreat from the second floor of the OK Hotel.

On May 10, 1894, Doolin and his gang rode into Southwest City, Missouri, and dismounted behind the town's post office and tied up their horses. According to the Southwest City *Enterprise* quoted in the Neosho *Times* on May 17, 1894, "Three of them made their way immediately to the bank while the other four took positions, two in the pool hall...and...two stood in Doctor Nichols' yard...."

The *Enterprise* reported that the robbers gave the "order for everybody to hunt holes, accompanied by an oath. To give their language more force, they began firing their winchesters, and kept up a fusillade."

While guns were being trained upon A.F. Ault, the bank owner, and his assistant, Mr. Snyder, a couple of the outlaws "crawled through the cashier's window."

The crooks snatched up all the money they could find in the vault and cashier's drawer, and crammed it in a sack and headed for their mounts and their getaway "keeping up a constant firing at every one who dared to show his head."

Meanwhile, outside in the street, the four "were doing deadly execution with their winchesters." They were buying precious time for their cohorts in the bank with their hot lead.

The bandits made off with about $3,700, but not before they wounded J.C. Seabourne, an ex-State Senator, his brother, Oscar,

M.V. Hembree, and Deputy U.S. Marshal Simpson Melton. It was reported that a total of "100 shots were fired on Main Street and sounded like war times, and many citizens had very close calls from the robbers' guns."

As the Doolin gang turned south on Broadway they received a "warm reception" by City Marshal Carlyle, D.E. Havens, G.W. Smith, E.W. Eslinger and S. Melton; Charles Franks and Dick Prater also dished out a "dose as they passed the Baptist Church."

As a result of the gunplay, J.C. Seabourne did not recover but died a few days later. Oscar survived but Hembree lost his foot above the ankle.

The gang stopped about 14 miles south of Southwest City, took care of their wounds and had something to eat. It was later ascertained that six of the seven bandits were injured during the shoot-out and getaway.

The crime spree continued without Arkansas Tom and after the Rock Island train robbery near Dover, Oklahoma, Doolin decided he needed to recuperate, so he headed to Eureka Springs, Arkansas to enjoy the benefits of the healing bath waters located there. By this time, however, a trio of marshals had been sent out by Isaac Parker who was known as the "Hanging Judge" of Fort Smith, Ark.; the "Three Guardsmen" were made up of Chris Madsen, Heck Thomas and Bill Tilghman. On January 15, 1896, Marshall Tilghman arrested Doolin at a bathhouse in Eureka Springs. He was returned to Oklahoma and incarcerated awaiting trial. Not to be kept from his life of crime, Doolin masterminded a daring jailbreak on July 5, 1896, with several other prisoners and then went into hiding for awhile. Wanting to see his wife and son he risked riding back to his father-in-law's ranch to see them. On August 25, 1896, Bill Doolin was gunned down by Heck Thomas in a shoot-out near Lawson, Oklahoma. His riddled body was displayed on a mortuary slab and then buried in the Boot Hill section of Guthrie's Summit View Cemetery.

Such desperados as Bill Doolin made a name for themselves in the annals of American history, and are remembered for their lawlessness. The paths they traversed, for the most part, ended when the law finally caught up with them—as in Doolin's case. Their escapades live on as continual reminders of a time past and lessons learned along the trails of the Wild West.

BANK ROBBERY.

The Bank of Southwest City Robbed of $3,700.

[Southwest City Enterprise, Friday, May 11.]

At about 3:30 o'clock yesterday afternoon seven well armed men rode into town from the south and dismounted in the street, just back of the postoffice, and tied their horses. Three of them made their way immediately to the bank, while the other four took positions, two in the pool hall, just north and across the street from the postoffice, while the other two stood in Dr. Nichols' yard. The first words heard from them was an order for everybody to hunt holes, accompanied by an oath. To give their language more force they began firing their winchesters, and kept up a fusilade. The men proceeded to the bank, and covered Mr. Ault, the owner of the bank, and Mr. Snyder, an assistant, with revolvers. Two of the men immediately crawled through the cashier's window, while the third held revolvers on Mr Snyder and Mr. Ault. After relieving the vault and cashier's drawer of the money, they deposited it in a sack and made their way to their horses, keeping up a

Headlines from the Neosho *Times*, May 17, 1894.

Bill Doolin

Bibliography

Anderson, Dan, and Yadon, Laurence, *100 Oklahoma Outlaws, Gangsters, and Lawmen 1839-1939*, Pelican Publishing Company, 2007.

McNab, Chris, *Gunfighters: The Outlaws and Their Weapons*, Thunder Bay Press, San Diego, California, 2005.

Masterson, V.V., *The Katy Railroad and the Last Frontier*, The University of Oklahoma Press, 1952.

Turner, George, *Gun Fighters*, Baxter Lane Company, Amarillo, Texas, 1972.

Other Sources:

Southwest City History Centennial, McDonald County Library.
Southwest City *Enterprise*, May 11, 1894.
Neosho *Times*, May 17, 1894.

Blockade Hollow at Keetsville (Washburn), Missouri.

Battle at Keetsville: Blockade Hollow

IN THE NINETEENTH century scores of traces and trails meandered across the American landscape. Throughout the Civil War there were many significant battles and skirmishes along these paths which were recorded in official and county records. The Ozarks had a number of military actions and engagements, and Barry County, Missouri, was no stranger to the national struggle. One such place that was caught up in the chaos was the town of Keetsville (Washburn), located a few miles south of historic Cassville along what was once the Trail of Tears, Butterfield Overland Mail Stagecoach Route and the Old Wire Road.

About the region, *Goodspeed's Newton, Lawrence, Barry and McDonald Counties History* brags that "The prairie of the same name stretches out before this hamlet, while all around one of the finest agricultural regions in all the Southwest is to be seen." The area also has some deep valleys and steep terrain that played an unusual but important role during the War Between the States.

In 1840 Judge Cureton purchased the land where Keetsville would be located, but later sold it to J.T. Keet who laid out the town that took his name. However, during the Civil War Keetsville was destroyed. In 1868, three years after the Civil War, a new town rose out of the ashes and a petition was presented to change the name of Keetsville to Washburn—it was adopted. The town was later incorporated on August 4, 1880.

TRACES OF OZARKS PAST

Just north of Keetsville, the town of Cassville became the county seat after it was moved from McDowell in June, 1845. By 1861, Cassville had about 300 residents and on October 31, Missouri's Governor Claiborne Fox Jackson along with eleven senators and forty-four representatives assembled there to sign the "acts of secession from the United States and annexation to the Confederate States." This action would help to catapult the Cassville and Keetsville area into a state of turmoil for the remainder of the war.

The location of these towns on the Old Wire Road, which was heavily used for troop movements during the Civil War, delivered them into a constant path of difficulty. Also, on the south side of Keetsville was the Harbin Station, a stagecoach stop which had been used for the Butterfield Overland Mail before the outbreak of the war. The proximity of Keetsville kept its residents in constant dread and fear from Union and Confederate forces as well as from rogue guerrillas and bushwhackers. Keetsville was considered to have, for the most part, Southern sympathies and according to the *Official Records of the Union and Confederate Armies*, Union Colonel Clark Wright of the Sixth Missouri Cavalry, frustrated over the town and its people, wrote that: "It is the worst hole in all this country."

Keetsville never hosted any major engagements; however, one significant skirmish recorded in the *Official Records* occurred on February 25, 1862. Colonel Wright, reporting from Cassville on February 27th to Union Brigadier General Samuel R. Curtis, two days after the action, believed their control of Keetsville was threatened and gave this account of the battle: "About 11 o'clock on the night of the 25th some 500 mounted men, well armed, supposed to be Texas Rangers, made a descent upon their camp from the right and left through the brush, riding down the picket and guards, and commenced a general fire upon the men asleep in camp. The captain [Captain Samuel Montgomery] rallied his force on foot and a general fight ensued. A portion of our men, however, were cut off, but the remainder stood their ground and three times repulsed the enemy. After about twenty minutes, however, the enemy's superior force being about to surround our force, the captain fell back under cover of the brush and maintained his position and held the town, the enemy retiring."

Battle at Keetsville: Blockade Hollow

The Confederates had stampeded about 40 horses during the attack, and at Harbin Station just south of town, "they captured 10 prisoners, a sutler, and teamster, and burning three wagons before the door." Col. Wright reported that casualties were light on both sides as a result of the battle at Keetsville. Capt. Montgomery fell back to Cassville to acquire assistance, while the remainder of his forces stayed behind at the Keetsville battleground to collect property and bury the dead.

Citizens were believed to have been aware of the attack beforehand, and were thought to have "communicated intelligence to the enemy, and purposely kept all knowledge of it from Capt. Montgomery, and in the afternoon before the fight the ladies all left town, one at a time, and that at the time of the attack all were out; and many other circumstances [according to Col. Wright] prove conclusively that the citizens are to all intents and purposes a part of the attacking party, there being no exceptions."

In response to the Keetsville skirmish, Brig. Gen. Samuel R. Curtis writes on March 4th ordering Col. Wright to "drive the enemy that assailed him...Take care of the enemy in the vicinity of Keetsville, and see that trains are not interrupted." This response by Brig. Gen. Curtis helps to reveal the importance of Keetsville and Cassville on the Old Wire Road.

Brig. Gen. Curtis also goes on to report in the *Official Records* his opinion and judgment concerning some of Keetsville's population, saying that: "There is a great set of rogues about Keetsville, and I hope you will find and arrest and send back the most of them."

One tale is told in *Goodspeed's History of Barry County* about a time when Capt. Montgomery was resting at the residence of an old lady, Mrs. Walker, who was unaware of who he was, which went like this: "I hear old Montgomery had a close call at Keetsville, but I'm sorry they did not kill him," said Mrs. Walker.

To this Capt. Montgomery replied: "How did you hear this?"

"Oh," she said, "the woods are full of Federals, and they haven't sense enough to hold their tongues, but I wanted to hear that old Capt. Montgomery was killed, I did."

"Well," replied the Captain, "I'm old Montgomery."

TRACES OF OZARKS PAST

"Well," she boldly replied, "I have nothing to take back."

Another interesting action to occur in Keetsville, according to county history, is a military tactic that was used there which happened at a place known as "Blockade Hollow" located about a mile southeast of town. The hollow rises very abruptly on both sides creating an area where troops were known to have, while being pursued, delay their adversaries by cutting and felling timbers across or constructing a rocky barrier in the hollow. The obstructions allowed more time for troops to escape—Union or Confederate, due to Keetsville's Ozark terrain at Blockade Hollow.

Roads are sometimes nothing more than the means to travel from one place to another, but during the American Civil War they could cause a whirlwind of trouble and tribulation to anyone living along one of them. But, in the end, those lesser-known places like Keetsville are now respectfully remembered in the annals of Ozarks history.

Battle at Keetsville: Blockade Hollow

Bibliography

Jackson, Rex T., *Sleuthing Historic Keetsville*, The Ozarks Reader Magazine, Vol. 3, No. 2, 2006.

Goodspeed's History of Barry County, Goodspeed Publishing Company, 1888.

Official Records of the Union and Confederate Armies, Washington: Government Printing Office, 1881.

War Eagle Mill's 18-ft. undershot waterwheel.

War Eagle Mill

AS PIONEERS and early settlers ventured westward and first laid eyes upon the mountains, valleys and prairies that make up the Ozarks region, they could envision the "good life" feasting upon its rich bounties. Sights common to modern-day jigsaw puzzle pictures and greeting cards, the scenic Ozarks was indeed a treasure trove of plenty – timber, wild game, fruit, nuts, fertile farmland and rushing waters. Some of those newcomers also had the foresight to respect and realize the potential of the many rivers, streams and springs as a powerful energy source – and it didn't take long before they were harnessed.

In the 19th century and early 20th century many water mills were constructed and operated throughout the Ozarks. By the middle of the 20th century, however, most water mills were closed. In recent years, the restoration and preservation of some of these rustic monuments of that era have increased. They have become tourist destinations, historical attractions and have even been converted into homes.

Early on, the need for grinding corn, wheat, lumber and other things was established and many millwrights set to work constructing, for the most part, "undershot" and "overshot" mills using a variety of natural water sources. The location often determined the type of mill that would be built. Sometimes dams were needed to divert water to the mill race and power an undershot waterwheel, while an overshot wheel might be turned by channeling water from a hillside spring gushing out above the mill site. In many cases "turbines" later replaced the mill's waterwheel. Mills that had a pair of millstones available for grinding, one for flour and the other for cornmeal, was preferred, since the condition of the stone's surface was effected by the type of grain the stone was repeatedly used for; corn has a oily exudation that penetrates the surface of the millstone which makes it less suitable for wheat. The hand "dressing" of millstones was an art that required a bit of skill. The stone's surface was called a "land" and the grooves cut into it were called "furrows". The distance between the two grinding stones needed to be carefully monitored during the milling process. The old saying "keeping your nose to the grindstone" came from this part of a miller's work.

The establishment of a water mill would bring business and activity which many times spawned towns and communities. People would come from all over the surrounding countryside with wagon loads of grain and logs. The miller would generally charge a fee or take a percentage of the job.

The beauty and tranquility of Ozark mills continues to educate and inspire the modern world. The wisdom of harnessing the free power and energy of water in times past is sensible to modern demands, as well. The importance of the water mill was such that during the American Civil War mills were utilized by both the Union and the Confederacy. And for this reason, they were also burnt to the ground on occasion to keep an opposing army from taking the liberty of using them.

One of the most popular and most photographed water mills in the Ozarks is War Eagle Mill, located a few miles east of Rogers, Arkansas in Benton County. Situated on the bank of War Eagle River next to a steel, wood-planked bridge, War Eagle Mill is an iconic example of the milling era.

In the 1830s a man named Sylvanus Blackburn migrated from Tennessee to the Ozarks. Along the War Eagle River in northern Arkansas' mountainous region, he put down his roots and began to clear the rocky land and build a log cabin. Knowing that the river could supply ample power, Blackburn constructed a water-powered grist mill that served well until it was destroyed by a flood in 1848.

Blackburn got busy and rebuilt a four-story mill not long afterwards and its importance gained the attention of "Billy Yank" and "Johnny Reb" during the War Between the States.

In early March, 1862, the area was a "tender box" of military activity massing for a significant engagement at nearby Pea Ridge, Arkansas, a few miles northwest of War Eagle Mill. The Battle of Pea Ridge occurred on March 7-8, but a few days before, troops passing through would make a raid on War Eagle Mill that would make Sylvanus Blackburn's worst fear come to pass.

On March 2, 1862, Blackburn's handiwork was torched, and in the *Official Records of the Union and Confederate Armies* its abandonment and possible demise was discussed in a report made by Union Colonel E.A. Carr dated February 28, 1862, saying: "Colonel Dodge came in this morning with all the men and teams he had at the Eagle Mills; he regretted very much to leave them, and says the inhabitants begged him to stay. Blackburn, the owner, is very fearful the mills will be burned.

"The Texans camped not far from the mills, both going and returning.

"Dodge says that there are but two passages through the country from Huntsville towards Crossville, one by Blackburn's and the other by Van Winkle's 3 miles off...."

A few days later on March 3, 1862, Union Brigadier General Samuel R. Curtis who was encamped in the area made a report concerning the mill's fiery fate, and said: "The mill run by Colonel Dodge – Blackman's [Blackburn] Mill, 16 miles southeast of this place – was burned last night by the rebels, and they also burned considerable forage in that region."

And again on March 4, 1862, Brig. Gen. Curtis reported that: "...They burned Blackman's [Blackburn] Mill, a fine one...night before last, and were burning all the forage in that region. Have sent a force to rout them, with directions to go as far as Huntsville if superior force does not check me. The Indian regiments have joined the enemy at Boston Mountains. The only strong point to entrench is Sugar Creek, and Cross Timber, beyond this. Cross Hollow is easily turned by an open campaign country a little west of the crossing.

"Sugar Creek Hollow extends for miles, a gorge, with rough, precipitate sides, the road crossing it at nearly right angles. I shall keep an outpost here and in the vicinity of Bentonville, with pickets and patrols still farther south. Forage is becoming scarce by the consumption of my troops and the burning by the enemy. Nothing could be more injurious to the country than this burning of mills...."

After the war, in 1873, James Austin Cameron Blackburn, Sylvanus' son, rebuilt the mill again – it bustled with activity until it burned in 1924. It would end the Blackburn's association with War Eagle Mill.

Finally, in 1973, the fourth War Eagle Mill was erected on the original site by Jewell A. and Leta Medlin and Zoe Medlin Caywood – and milling resumed.

Water mills once dotted the landscape, and signs of their existence can still be seen in many places throughout the Ozarks—stalwart examples of bygone contributors of power. In the case of the War Eagle Mill, its location left it vulnerable during the Civil War on a path to its fiery demise.

War Eagle Mill

Bibliography

Jackson, Rex T., *War Eagle: The Official Reports on the Abandonment and Burning of Blackburn's Mill*, The Ozarks Reader Magazine, Vol. 3, No. 3, 2006.

Larkin, David, *Mill: The History and Future of Naturally Powered Buildings*, Universe Publishing, 2000.

Other Sources:

War Eagle Mill
The Official Records of the Union and Confederate Armies, Washington: Government Printing Office, 1881.

Above: A mural in Granby, Mo. Below: Henry T. Blow's final resting place at Bellefontaine Cemetery in St. Louis. (Photos by the author.)

Granby Mining "Stampede"

IN THE 1800s, Southwest Missouri bustled with mining activity and many communities throughout the region swelled in population. In *The Ozarks Region: Its History and Its People*, it confirms the 1887 mining boom in the town of Aurora: "Strangers poured in from all over the world. They bought town lots and leased land. Many built houses, others tented in the suburbs. Those with means purchased ground and went to prospecting. Mining plants sprang into existence and the song of the busy miner, and the movement of the numerous hand-jigs and other crude devices told of the developing mining interests...."

Early in 1849, David Campbell was first to find lead in Joplin, Mo., and shortly after in 1850, Madison Vickory made the same discovery in Granby, Mo. However, it wasn't until about 1853 that William Foster began to mine a significant amount of lead at Granby. By 1854, miners pour-in and Granby began to grow by leaps and bounds and the "stampede" of new residents increased Granby's population to about 8,000 by 1859. *Goodspeed's 1888 History of McDonald and Newton Counties* reported that: "Johnson's, Plumber's, Livingston's and Long's furnaces were running at full blast, and the hills and vales were literally covered with prospectors."

Mining continued and Granby City prospered until the outbreak of the American Civil War. All of the mining ceased by 1862 and the war left Granby unpopulated, except for the lead taken by the Confederacy to produce bullets. *Goodspeed* confirms the fact: "...much of the lead which found a resting-place in the bodies of Union troops was manufactured here [Granby] into bullets for small arms."

The importance of mining lead at Granby during the Civil War made it a military objective. It would, on several occasions, become drawn into the war. This was the case in the fall of 1862 a few days after the Southern victory at nearby Newtonia, Mo., on September 30. Confederate Lieutenant Colonel M.W. Buster, commander of the Indian Battalion under Colonel Douglas H. Cooper's First Brigade of the Trans-Mississippi Department, reported in the *Official Records of the Union and Confederate Armies*, that: "On...October 3, [1862] I was ordered with my command and Major Bryan's (whole force of about 400 men) to proceed to and occupy the town of Granby...reaching that place at 6:30 p.m. Finding water scarce, marched the whole command to Shoal Creek, distant 1 ¼ miles. Directed Captain McDonel to take his company and guard the road at the creek which led out of Granby on the left in a northwest direction, with instructions to place pickets beyond. I also placed a company from Bryan's battalion on the same creek on a road leading out of town to the right with like instructions regarding pickets, and left Major Bryan's on the main Sarcoxie road leading out of Granby to the northward with the balance of his battalion, at the same time instructing him to keep his outposts strongly guarded, and in case of an attack to annoy the enemy as much as possible and to fall back in order on the reserve, which I marched back to Granby, and occupied the town as my military headquarters."

About 2 o'clock that morning, October 4, 1862, "considerable firing" was heard from the direction of Major Bryan's encampment. A courier was sent back to Lieut. Col. Buster's Confederate headquarters in Granby with the message that "they had encountered the enemy, their advance firing into our pickets and ours returning it...reporting the enemy to be in force and with artillery...."

As a result of the Union's assault, Major Bryan ordered a retreat

Granby Mining "Stampede"

and fell back to Granby where Lieut. Col. Buster immediately formed his men into column and moved toward the oncoming Federals on the main Sarcoxie road—about a quarter of a mile from Granby. When they met the advancing Federals, both sides poured in a volley "and the firing became general and rapid...."

Lieut. Buster found it difficult to form his men into line because of the dense, thick underbrush and the darkness of the night. They were eventually forced to fall back upon Granby once more, "finding by the sound of the enemy's bugle" they were being flanked.

After falling back an additional half a mile, the sun was rising and it began a pouring rain, but in spite of it all, Lieut. Buster admitted that: "This was a time that tried the material of which my command was composed, and it is with more than pride that I say a more determined set of officers and soldiers it never was my pleasure to ride before and look upon. Not a soldier in the whole line but exposed himself to shelter his gun from the weather."

That same day, Union General John M. Schofield's division along with General James G. Blunt's division and General Totten's Missourians, each about 6,000 strong, entered Confederate-held Newtonia and drove "the enemy out under the fire of cannon."

Brigadier General Schofield reported that "a running artillery fight of about two hours' duration" ensued with "only trifling loss on either side." For the time being, the lead had ceased to fly in Granby.

In 1865, when the Civil War was over, Henry Taylor Blow, Peter E. Blow, James B. Eads, Barton Bates and Charles K. Dickson of St. Louis would organize the Granby Mining and Smelting Company. This company of St. Louisans would make Missouri mining history.

Henry Blow, the president of the company, was born in Southampton County, Virginia, on July 15, 1817. He moved to St. Louis, Missouri when he was 13-years-old and went on to attend the St. Louis University for a couple of years. Blow practiced law for awhile but eventually went into business with his brother manufacturing and selling drugs, paints and oils. Overtime, he began to get interested in lead mining—and, as a result, established the Granby Mining and Smelting Company with the help of prominent friends like James B. Eads who built ironclad gunboats for the North during the Civil War, the first steel bridge over the Mississippi River (St. Louis), and jetties at the mouth of the Mississippi among other things.

As for Blow, he served as president of the Iron Mountain Railroad and oversaw much of the construction of the railway. In the fall of 1861, President Abraham Lincoln honored him with the Belgian mission. A year later he was elected to the United States Senate where he served the Thirty-eighth and Thirty-ninth Congress. Blow also went on to be nominated to the Brazilian mission until his health began to falter. In 1873 he returned to his hometown of St. Louis and for his last public service he was appointed as a member of the Board of Commissioners for the District of Columbia.

Henry T. Blow died at Saratoga Springs, New York, on September 11, 1875, and he was buried at Bellefontaine Cemetery in St. Louis. The St. Louis *Globe Democrat* had this to say about his passing: "No death among the many whose names are intimately linked with the social and material history and progress of this community could occasion a more profound sorrow than that of Hon. Henry Blow...."

Even the New York *Times* felt the need to weight-in on the death of Henry Blow and confessed that: "His death will be mourned in many places, for he was widely known and universally loved and respected."

About the success of the Granby mines, in the *Centennial History of Newton County, Missouri*, it boasted: "The furnaces generally are by far the largest and most complete of any in the State, and perhaps the largest in the world, and they usually have to run night and day to perform the work required of them."

In the Granby *Miner*, January 10, 1874, it proudly proclaimed to its readers" "Who says Granby is not improving more than any other town in the Southwest."

Much of Granby's progress can be attributed to Henry Blow. The New York *Times* went so far as to say that his contributions and interest in the lead mines of Missouri "may be said to have built up the flourishing City of Granby, in the south-west part of the State."

By the end of World War II, however, the lead deposits in Granby were depleted, and likewise, the one-time boomtown decreased in size and activity. The "stampede" was over and the Ozark town of Granby returned to normalcy. But the work of Henry Blow and the Granby mining era is not forgotten there, and the signs of those times still linger.

Granby, Mo., water tower reads: "Oldest Mining Town in the Southwest."

Granby Mining "Stampede"

Bibliography

Amcler, Kevin, *Final Resting Place: The Lives and Deaths of Famous St. Louisans*, Virginia Publishing Company, St. Louis, Missouri, 1997.

Jackson, Rex T., *A Southwestern Missouri Mining Boomtown Hosts A Civil War Battle*, The Ozarks Reader Magazine, Vol. 4, No. 2, 2007. *Henry Taylor Blow and the Granby Stampede*, The Ozarks Reader Magazine, Vol. 6, No. 3, 2009.

Other Sources:

Goodspeed's History of McDonald and Newton Counties, 1888.

New York *Times*, September 12, 1875.

Official Records of the Union and Confederate Armies, Washington: Government Printing Office, 1881.

Springfield, Missouri: Interstate Historical Society, *The Ozarks Region: Its History and Its People*, Volume 2, 1917.

St. Louis *Globe Democrat*, September 12, 1875.

Zagonyi Marker just west of Kansas Expressway
on Mt. Vernon Street, Springfield, Missouri.

Zagonyi's Brave Springfield Cavalry Charges

AFTER THE Union's early Civil War defeats at Carthage, Wilson's Creek, Dry Wood and Lexington, Missouri, Major-General John C. Fremont, ordered Major Charles Zagonyi and the Fremont Body Guard to Springfield, Mo. Major Gen. Fremont, commanding the Headquarters Western Department was determined "to clear the State entirely of the enemy...."

J.H. Eaton, Acting Assistant Adjutant-General, reporting in the *Official Records of the Union and Confederate Armies* on October 26, 1861, states that in "addition to Zagonyi's 150 of the guard, Major [Frank J.] White had joined him with about 180 mounted men." However, Maj. Zagonyi would later fail to mention Maj. White's troops in the action. A couple of impatient reports about this "gross injustice" are included in the *Official Records*, dated November 12 and December 18, 1861, by Patrick Naughton, Captain Irish Dragoons, Twenty-third Illinois Volunteers.

According to Maj. Zagonyi, he arrived in Springfield on October 25, 1861, and after detouring about 5 miles to the west side of town near the Mount Vernon Road, he found the Confederates "in their old camp" and quickly came upon them "drawn up in line of battle" as he "emerged from the wood near the Mount Vernon road."

Zagonyi was unable to form his men for battle because the "place was too confined." He had to travel about 250 yards down a lane and make a charge in their camp. Zagonyi reported that: "My men belonging to the Body-Guard amounted to 150, and were exposed from the moment we entered the lane to a murderous crossfire...Half of my command charged upon the infantry and the remainder upon the cavalry, breaking their line at every point."

Zagonyi's men attempted to follow the Confederate infantry into the thick underbrush but were unable to do so with any success. According to Zagonyi "the cavalry fled in all directions through the town. I rallied, and charged through the streets in all directions about twenty times, clearing the town and neighborhood, returning at last to the court-house, where I raised the flag of one of my companies, liberated the prisoners, and united my men, which amounted to 70, the rest being scattered or lost."

A reported number of about 2,000 to 2,200 Confederate troops were thought to be encamped in the area when Zagonyi arrived, and he later recalled that: "They gave me a very warm reception—warmer than I expected." Since it was growing dark and Zagonyi's men were exhausted from the march—there, and the vigorous battle, they retired and set about collecting the wounded and picking up the dead.

About his troops, Zagonyi said that he had "seen battles and cavalry charges before, but never imagined that a body of men could endure and accomplish so much in the face of such a fearful disadvantage. At the cry of 'Fremont and the Union,' which was raised at every charge, they dashed forward repeatedly in perfect order with resistless energy."

And in another place, Zagonyi writes: "I have seen charges, but such brilliant unanimity and bravery I have never seen and did not expect it. Their war cry, 'Fremont and the Union,' broke forth as thunder."

About Maj. White's 180 mounted rangers, Zagonyi stated that they "left me at the beginning of the action...before my first charge, and I saw no more of them until the next day."

Captain Naughton later complained: "Gross injustice has been done to my company in the report of Major Zagonyi."

The success of the Zagonyi charges were no doubt made possible by, not only bravery, but by their use of superior arms—rifles and revolvers. The Southern forces were equipped with only muzzleloaders and shotguns.

As a result, the Zagonyi operation offered the Union a satisfying taste of significant Civil War victory in Missouri after their earlier defeats. For further gratification, however, Zagonyi must have also savored the victory flag he raised over Springfield as they stopped and rested after that eventful fall day to lick their wounds.

Bibliography

Jackson, Rex T., *Zagonyi's Daring Springfield Civil War Cavalry Charges*, The Ozarks Reader Magazine, Vol. 4, No. 3, 2007.

Other Sources:

Official Records of the Union and Confederate Armies, Washington: Government Printing Office, 1881.

Zagonyi Marker, University Club Historic Marker No. 17, Mt. Vernon Street, Springfield, Missouri.

The Elkhorn Tavern at the Pea Ridge National Battlefield, near Pea Ridge, Arkansas.

Tomahawking and Scalping in the Ozarks

IN 1861 at the outbreak of the War Between the States, division and hot-button issues plagued the nation. The differences that existed eventually pitted brother against brother beginning with the bombardment of Fort Sumter on April 14, 1861; followed by the *first* significant land battle of the Civil War at Carthage, Missouri, on July 5, 1861—eleven days before the 1st Battle of Manassas (or Bull Run).

After these actions the war continued with a host of great, bloody engagements; as well as many skirmishes and other clashes of arms both east and west of the Mississippi River. There were also battles fought in the Gulf, along the coastlines and on the inland waterways with wooden ships, ironclad gunboats, and experimental underwater vessels (submarines); all for the purpose of solving their differences militarily.

One lesser-known strategic military practice during the Civil War, however, was the use of Native American tribes recently relocated by force to Indian Territory (Oklahoma). The mustering in of Native Americans in the War Between the States was pursued vigorously by both the Union and the Confederacy. And their participation in that war was controversial. A large number of Creek, Chickasaw, Choctaw, Cherokee, and Seminole, for the most part, would be enlisted to fight for the North and South in, not only the Indian Nations, but also in Missouri and Arkansas. Their work would be significant, but is nearly forgotten in the quagmire of

American history.

Because of early Confederate victories at Carthage, Manassas, and Wilson's Creek (fought near Springfield, Mo.), many Native Americans sided with the South; unhappy encounters with the Federal government might have also influenced their loyalties. Eventually, their participation in the Civil War would be reconsidered after the Battle of Pea Ridge—a history-making engagement in northern Arkansas that helped to decide the future of Missouri.

Union troops under Major General Samuel R. Curtis and Brigadier General Franz Sigel, and the Confederation of Major General Earl Van Dorn, Major General Sterling Price, Brig. Gen. Ben McCulloch, and Indian troops under Brig. Gen. Albert Pike were massing to face-off in the vicinity of the Elkhorn Tavern located near Pea Ridge, Arkansas. General Curtis' forces were digging in along the frozen, Ozark bluffs of Sugar Creek near the Tavern.

In the *Official Records of the Union and Confederate Armies,* Union Gen. Curtis describes the landscape in this way: "The hills are high on both sides, and the main road from Fayetteville [Arkansas] by Cross Hollow to Keetsville [Washburn, Missouri] intercepts the valley nearly at right angles. The road from Fayetteville by Bentonville [Arkansas] to Keetsville is quite a detour, but it also comes up the Sugar Creek Valley; a branch, however, takes off and runs nearly parallel to the main or Telegraph Road, some 3 miles from it. The Sugar Creek Valley, therefore, intercepts all these roads."

The Southerners and Federals would clash here in the Battle of Pea Ridge (or Elkhorn Tavern) on March 7-8, 1862, where about 1,000 men on each side would be killed or wounded. Left on the bloody Pea Ridge battleground, however, there were mangled, mutilated and scalped Union soldiers discovered—believed to be the handiwork of Gen. Albert Pike's Indian troops.

It was in these beautiful Ozark hills and hollows of northern Arkansas where an American, homegrown conflict was waged; it included a Confederate Indian regiment of Cherokee Colonel (later Brig. Gen.) Stand Watie and an Indian regiment of Colonel John

Drew. And in the *Official Records* of Brig. Gen. Albert Pike dated March 14, 1862, he is well-known to historians for having said: "...let them [(Indians)] join in the fight in their own fashion." He would later be admonished for this decision.

After hearing about scalped and mutilated Federals on the field after the battle, Gen. Pike summoned his surgeon and assistant-surgeon to investigate the matter, General Pike issued an order, and in it he denounced the ghastly practice. According to Pike, some of the Indians which perpetrated the act were in Brig. Gen. Ben McCulloch's corps on the first day of battle. And according to Wiley Britton's *Union and Confederate Indians in the Civil War* found in *Battles and Leaders of the Civil War*, he writes that: "...the scalping was done at night in a quarter of the field not occupied by the Indian troops under his immediate command."

The nation was outraged about the incident and in the New York *Tribune*, March 27, 1862, they had nothing good to say about "...Albert Pike who led the Aboriginal Corps of Tomahawkers and Scalpers at the battle of Pea Ridge."

The *Official Records* offer dialog back and forth between Union Gen. Curtis and Confederate Gen. Earl Van Dorn. On March 9, 1862, Curtis orders up a letter to be fired at Van Dorn, and says: "The general regrets that we find on the battle-field, contrary to civilized warfare, many of the Federal dead who were tomahawked, scalped, and their bodies shamefully mangled, and expresses a hope that this important struggle may not degenerate to a savage warfare."

Van Dorn's Assistant Adjutant-General returned his reply to Curtis on March 14, 1862, and said: "He is pained to learn by your letter brought to him by the commanding officer of the party that the remains of some of your soldiers have been reported to you to have been scalped, tomahawked, and otherwise mutilated.

"He hopes you have been misinformed with regard to this matter, the Indians who formed part of his forces having for many years been regarded as civilized people. He will, however, most cordially unite with you in repressing the horrors of this unnatural war, and that you may co-operate with him to this end more effectually he desires me to inform you that many of our men who surrendered themselves prisoners of war were reported to him as having been murdered in cold blood by their captors, who were alleged to be Germans.

"The general commanding feels sure that you will do your part, as he will, in preventing such atrocities in future, and that the perpetrators of them will be brought to justice, whether German or Choctaw."

Another report made by Adjutant John W. Noble to Maj. Gen. Curtis, found that, after an investigation concerning the atrocities committed on the Pea Ridge battlefield, concluded the following: "The killed were buried...after the battle was over and pursuit ended. Hearing it reported by my men that several of the killed had been found scalped, I had the dead exhumed, and on personal examination I found that it was a fact beyond dispute that 8 of the killed showed unmistakable evidence that the men had been murdered after they were wounded; that first having fallen in the charge from bullet wounds, they were afterwards pierced through the heart and neck with knives by a savage and relentless foe...."

About the armament of the Indian troops, John H. Lawson reported in the *Official Records* that he "saw about 2,000 Indians, said to be under the command of Albert Pike and Martin Green, marching towards the battle-ground in good order. These were all mounted, armed with shot-guns, rifles, and large knives."

For the most part, it was decided after the Battle of Pea Ridge that the Indian troops would be confined to military operations in Indian Territory for the remainder of the Civil War on account of the outrages. This official report concerning their redeployment was sent to Brig. Gen. Albert Pike: "It is not expected that you will give battle to a large force, but by felling trees, burning bridges, removing supplies of forage and subsistence, attacking his trains, stampeding his animals, cutting off his detachments, and other similar means, you will be able materially to harass his army...please endeavor to restrain them from committing any barbarities upon the wounded, prisoners, or dead who may fall into their hands...."

Native Americans would, nevertheless, be used several months later by both the North and the South on September 30, 1862, at the

1st Battle of Newtonia in southwest Missouri—the first time that Indian troops would face each other in America's Civil War. And in *The American Indian as Participant in the Civil War* by Annie Heloise Abel, concerning Newtonia, she wrote about the ongoing incidents that occurred there which continued to shock the nation: "Their discipline had yet left much to be desired. Scalping of the dead took place as on the battle-field of Pea Ridge...."

Native Americans continued to be used to some degree throughout the Civil War, but their contributions were more acceptable in their own territory at such significant battles as: 1st and 2nd Cabin Creek; Round Mountain; Bird Creek; Patriot Hills; Fort Wayne; Honey Springs; Flat Rock and on many other occasions.

Annie Heloise Abel writes, concerning the use of Native Americans, that the "Federals and Confederates had alike resorted to it for purposes other than the red man's own." Nevertheless, by the end of the Civil War Indian Territory was a wasteland of blackened fields, forests and burned-out homes and schools.

In the end, the War Between the States did little to help struggling Native Americans recover from their recent relocations to the Nations. Most of their hard work was lost, and once again they were forced to pick-up what was left of their torn lives and rebuild. Their actions in the Civil War will forever be an important piece of American and Ozarks past.

An artillery battery at the Pea Ridge National Battlefield, near Pea Ridge, Arkansas.

Bibliography

Abel, Annie Heloise, *The American Indian as Participant in the Civil War*, Arthur H. Clark Company, Cleveland, 1919.

Britton, Wiley, *Union and Confederate Indians in the Civil War*, Battles and Leaders of the Civil War, The Century Company, 1887.

Jackson, Rex T., *Native Americans Mustered into the Civil War: Ozark Tomahawking and Scalping*, The Ozarks Reader Magazine, Vol. 7, No. 3, 2010.

Other Sources:

Official Records of the Union and Confederate Armies, Washington: Government Printing Office, 1881.

A Civil War monument at the I.O.O.F. Cemetery in Neosho, Missouri.

Capturing Neosho: Secession in the Ozarks

AFTER CAMP JACKSON, which was located near St. Louis, Missouri, fell to Captain Nathaniel Lyon commanding the Union's Second Infantry on May 10, 1861; it prompted the beginning of Missouri Governor Claiborne Fox Jackson's retreat toward the extreme southern part of the state near Confederate Arkansas. The retreat would eventually bring Governor Jackson to the towns of Neosho and Cassville in the fall of 1861, and as a result, forever highlight them in the annals of America's Civil War history.

In the summer of that year, Neosho was under control of Union Captain Joseph Conrad, Third Missouri Infantry. Capt. Conrad had nearly 100 men and had taken precautions to safeguard the town with sentinels and around-the-clock patrols. Unbeknownst to Capt. Conrad and his small force, about 1,500 Confederates under Colonel Churchill and Major McIntosh (Arkansas Rangers) were moving in from the west and south side of Neosho on July 5, 1861, and were preparing an assault.

McIntosh had in all, "four companies of Colonel Churchill's regiment of Arkansas Mounted Riflemen and Captain Caroll's regiment of Arkansas State troops to make an attack" on the Federals at Neosho, "in conjunction with Colonel Churchill, commanding six companies of his regiment."

In the *Official Records of the Union and Confederate Armies*, Capt. James McIntosh writes that he dismounted "four companies of

Churchill's regiment about a quarter of a mile of the town, and marched them by platoon at double-quick within 200 yards of the Court-House, where [he] found a company 80 strong...."

Capt. Conrad reported hearing a "cannonading" at about 11 o'clock, after which he "dispatched a patrol of 20 men under Lieutenant Damde." About two hours later Lieut. Damde returned, and after a few minutes had passed, "the enemy came pouring in in all directions" which left Capt. Conrad with a very difficult decision to make, he writes: "Finding it impossible for me to hold my post with success, after due deliberation, after due consultation with my officers and men, I concluded it would be best to make the surrender as it was required—namely, unconditionally."

After the Southerners had overwhelmed the Federal post, Capt. McIntosh demanded surrender and graciously gave Conrad and his men ten minutes to make up their minds. McIntosh wrote: "At the end of the time the captain in command made an unconditional surrender of the company, laying down their arms and side-arms." According to McIntosh they "took 100 rifles with saber bayonets, a quantity of ammunition, and a train of seven wagons loaded with provisions." Neosho had fallen to the Confederacy.

"The officers and men," according to McIntosh, "did everything in their power to make the movement as prompt as possible, and they marched up to within a short distance of a force whose numbers were unknown with a step as regular and a front as unbroken as a body of veterans."

The Federals were rounded-up and held in the courthouse for three days. Capt. Conrad reported in the *Official Records* that "the officers of the Arkansas Rangers, as well as the Missouri troops, behaved themselves quietly, accommodating, and friendly, both towards myself and men; but their privates on the contrary, in the most insulting and brutal manner."

They were finally released on the 8th, "having before given...parole of honor not to serve any more against the Confederate States of America during the war," and for their safety, they were escorted out of town by about 30 men. Conrad wrote about the dangers facing him and his men, saying: "...the people of Neosho and farmers of that vicinity [have] threatened to kill us in the streets."

Furthermore, Conrad, in recounting their exodus from Neosho, wrote: "After innumerable hardships and danger, without food and water, our canteens having been stolen from us by the Southern troops, we at last reached Springfield, my men all broken down, having traveled the distance of 85 miles in fifty hours, with hardly any food at all."

On July 11, 1861, a few days after Neosho fell to the South, Union Colonel Franz Sigel wrote to Brigadier General Sweeny, Commanding Southwest Expedition, and informed him of the loss of the post: "It is with the deepest regret that I must report the surprise and capture of Captain Conrad and his company of 94 men at Neosho on the 5th of July. Officers and men were released on oath not to bear arms against the Confederate States during the war."

Not long after the Confederacy gained control of Neosho, pro-Southern Governor Jackson arrived in the area. Gov. Jackson writing from Carthage, Mo., to Confederate President Jefferson Davis, dated October 12, 1861, delivered this report of confidence: "In a few days I have every reason to hope the legislature will be in session, and as soon as this takes place an ordinance of secession will be overwhelmingly ratified by the people whenever they can vote upon it."

True to his word Gov. Jackson made his way even further south to Confederate-held Neosho and on October 21, 1861, an extra session convened. In *Battles and Biographies of Missourians* or the *Civil War Period of Our State* published in 1900, author W.L. Webb writes: "According to Governor Jackson's proclamation, the Legislature convened at Neosho, in Masonic Hall. It is said that only thirty-nine members of both houses were present...An ordinance of secession was passed, and senators and representatives were elected to the Confederate Congress." It might be of some interest to know that in Webb's book it offers a tin-type cut of Governor Jackson with a signature beneath the cut that "was taken from a bill of 'Jackson money,' or Missouri script, printed on a hand press at Neosho, Mo."

Confederate Major-General Sterling Price encamped near Neosho on Oct. 26, 1861, commented on the historic event taking place at Neosho, and said: "Our legislature is still in session in Neosho."

The Legislature would again reconvene a few days later on October 31, 1861, at nearby Cassville in Barry County and according to *Goodspeed's Newton, Lawrence, Barry and McDonald Counties History* published in 1888, the "ordinance of secession was rewritten...in the northeast corner room of the court-house, at Cassville...." The session at Cassville which included eleven senators and forty-four representatives ended on November 7, 1861.

That same day, General Price, now encamped on Indian Creek in McDonald County, reported: "Our legislature has been in session for the last two weeks, and has passed an ordinance of secession, besides electing delegates to the Confederate Congress."

There would be a number of battles and skirmishes fought throughout the American Civil War in the Neosho area; with victories for both the Blue and the Gray. But the luster the Southern government enjoyed in the Ozarks in the fall of 1861 at Neosho, and again at Cassville, would never again be recaptured or realized.

Bibliography

Jackson, Rex T., *Battle for Neosho: Secession in the Missouri Ozarks*, The Ozarks Reader Magazine, Vol. 5, No. 2, 2008.

Webb, W.L., *Battles and Biographies of Missourians, or the Civil War Period of Our State*, Hudson-Kimberly Publishing Company, Kansas City, Missouri, 1900.

Other Sources:

Goodspeed's Newton, Lawrence, Barry and McDonald Counties History, 1888.

Official Records of the Union and Confederate Armies, Washington: Government Printing Office, 1881.

SPRINGFIELD MOB LYNCHES NEGROES

Suspected Ravishers Hauled Through Streets by Crowd of Thousands, Hanged to Electric Tower in Center of Square and Bodies Afterward Burned — Populace, Unsated, Threatens to Return to Wrecked Jail and Hang Four Other Negroes.

Springfield, Mo., April 14. — Two negroes were hanged on an electric tower in the center of the square at 11 o'clock tonight and their bodies burned.

Fully 5,000 people went to the county jail about 9 o'clock and with telephone poles and sledge hammers litterally tore the jail to pieces.

Finally two negro suspects were dragged from the jail and taken to the center of the public square and hanged. It is fully a mile from the jail to the square, and the mob marched down one of the principal streets of the town, shouting and firing pistols.

Last night a girl named Mabel Ed., of the jail and cut off the gas, hop- have congregated in Springfield. It

Headlines from the Joplin *Daily Globe*, April 15, 1906.

Vigilante Lynching in the "Queen City of the Ozarks"

TRAILBLAZERS who meander through Ozarks past—can, in hindsight, profit from the historic records that have lingered along the traces—eye-opening lessons that can stir the mind. It is concerning these beneficial discoveries of the past that entice such history-hungry travelers to make this journey-effort.

Only 41 years after the American Civil War had ended, the "Queen City of the Ozarks" (Springfield, Missouri), considered a staunch supporter of the Union during the war, ironically, hosted a vigilante-style hanging of three helpless African Americans. The unspeakable horror of that unforgettable night of mob violence has forever tainted American and Ozarks history with this hideous outbreak of injustice and racial hatred. Even though this event can never be erased or wiped clean from the pages of history, its lessons can continue to inspire future generations—that such things could never happen again.

At the turn-of-the-century (1900), Springfield boasted about 25,000 citizens with about 2,000 or more being African American. During this time, schools, churches, businesses and social gathering was still, for the most part, segregated—equality in America was still a work in progress. The "Jim Crow" laws (a minstrel show that stereo typed African Americans as inferior and ignorant) required railroads, theaters and other places to have separate facilities marked

"Whites Only" and so on. Whites championed many riots, burnings and hangings, while blacks protested their second-class citizen status by boycotting such things as streetcar segregation in towns like Atlanta, Augusta, Mobile, Houston and New Orleans—but the separation continued.

Racial problems in nearby Monett, Joplin, Peirce (Pierce) City, and Rogers, Arkansas prompted a number of African Americans to migrate to Springfield. In the Joplin *Daily Globe*, April 15, 1906, it writes: "It is feared that they may be run out of here [Springfield] the same as in other cities, so bitter has become the feeling."

Anti-black sentiment had also been growing in Springfield, due in large part to crime. The Springfield *Leader*, April 15, 1906, reported that "Two dastardly murders—that of Rouark and T.M. Kinney, were attributed to them, and it is possibly a fact that this sentiment was increased by the production of Thomas Dixon's play 'The Clansman,' which was here only recently. Consequently the smoldering embers of hatred were [fanned] into something akin to a conflagration...when the news that Mable Edwards [Edmondson], a young girl, had been criminally assaulted by two negroes...."

Apparently, Mable and Charles Cooper were in a buggy in a secluded area of the city when they were held up by two masked men. Cooper was knocked-out and Mable was reported to have been "dragged from the buggy and ravished."

Even though the perpetrators of the crime wore masks, Cooper identified Horace Duncan and Fred Coker, who were African Americans, and they were arrested by authorities. After their white employer at Pickwick Livery gave Duncan and Coker an ironclad alibi, they were released; however, Charles Cooper filed robbery charges against Duncan and the two suspects were again arrested and incarcerated at the county jail.

Regardless of the number of crimes that whites had also committed in Springfield over the years, these crimes associated and attributed to blacks had spawned outrage and racial opportunity to act on hatred and prejudice.

Concerning the assault on Edwards and Cooper, according to the *Daily Globe*, Mable Edwards "stated positively that they [Duncan and Coker] were not her assailants." It mattered little to the growing sentiments blossoming in Springfield, which had to be appeased.

In the county jail, besides Duncan and Coker, there were other African Americans being held for various crimes. The *Leader* reported that a large mob was forming and was on its way to the county jail which was under Sheriff E.V. Horner and his deputies, and that the "leaders of the mob were...from Polk county in the vicinity of Bolivar. It was said that eight hundred men from that vicinity arrived in Springfield at nightfall, and soon got in touch with those of this city who had been talking of mobbing the negroes the day previous."

The ever increasing mob traveled down South Campbell Street, up Walnut Street and to Springfield's Public Square—and finally, down Boonville Street to the county jailhouse where Sheriff Horner was standing between them and their prize—Duncan and Coker. The crowd demanded that he "give up" the two men, however, "Sheriff Horner refused and told the mob to be careful and not get the wrong man...where upon the leaders flourished their ropes, and in the vilest of language informed the sheriff that they would not be refused."

The angry mob then secured sledge hammers, telephone poles and other tools of demolition to gain entry into the jail cells. The fate of Duncan and Coker was sealed.

The *Globe* reported that "Sheriff Horner tried to argue with the mob, but it was determined, and hooted and insulted him. Jailer King was assaulted when he refused to give up the keys. He finally gave the mob some keys which were not for the cells and the mob was forced to smash in the iron bars.

"Besides the damage at the jail the mob all but wrecked the residence of Sheriff Horner. Doors were broken down, windows were smashed, furniture was demolished, pictures were torn from the walls and the sheriff's wife was rendered unconscious by fright and violence."

By this time the mob had swelled to thousands, who fired shots and roared a "constant howl." Eventually, a fire was started under the jail but failed to do much damage. All the while the sounds of "hammers and picks" were at work inside the jailhouse to reach the shocked, frightened men trapped within.

Finally, the work paid-off and the cells were thrust opened to their mass hatred and madness. They quickly secured their ropes "around the necks of the negroes and they were brought out of the jail through the windows...and the negroes were soon on the outside.

" 'To the square,' some leader of the mob shouted, and the great crowd started in that direction...By the time the negroes reached the square every available nook and window was filled with people...."

The *Globe's* headline read: "SPRINGFIELD MOB LYNCHES NEGROES. Suspected Ravishers Hauled Through Streets by Crowd of Thousands...." Duncan and Coker, according to the *Globe*, "were dragged from the jail and taken to the center of the public square and hanged. It is fully a mile from the jail to the square, and the mob marched down one of the principle streets of the town, shouting and firing pistols."

Someone in the crowd shouted "Shoot them full of holes," but because of the danger of hitting their vigilante comrades they decided to douse the condemned men, now dangling from the electric light tower on the town's square, with coal oil and set them on fire—which they did without any signs of mercy. It was about 11 o'clock at night. To make sure their morbid pleasure was fully realized, "Goods boxes were brought from all the stores around the square where they could be secured, and soon a great fire was raging which burned the negroes completely up, while the mob still howled its satisfaction." Torture, on this spring night in the Ozarks, had somehow become tolerated and acceptable.

The hideous attraction didn't stop there; they returned to the jailhouse and snatched up William Allen, a young African American. The Springfield *Republican* revealed how the mob was "overcome with their orgy and filled with exultant frenzy over their success," as they again rejoined the activities at the center of the city square. Allen was hung like Duncan and Coker, coated in coal oil and set ablaze. Before long, however, the rope had burned through and broke and his young body fell into the corpse-filled ashes below.

The *Daily Globe* had this to say about the event: "When daylight broke upon the scene there remained only the blackened trunks and charred remains of three negroes.

"Five thousand persons saw the trio hanged and burned. Among the crowd of spectators were hundreds of women and children, girls and boys."

It was also reported that onlookers even took souvenirs of bits of rope, clothes and bone from the ghastly rubble. On the very next day, Easter Sunday, thousands returned to the scene-of-the-crime dressed in their finest—men, women and children, to reminisce, gape and converse about the race-filled horror that had graced the heart of their city.

The National Guard was eventually brought in to restore order and Springfield was placed under martial law while the town's mayor delivered this proclamation: "To the people of Springfield: Excitement incident to the deplorable event which transpired in our city last Saturday night is subsiding, and quiet has been restored.

"As Mayor of your city, I call upon every citizen to assist in promoting peace and good order by refraining from inflammatory remarks or reckless criticism, whether in public or private. I recommend also to the people of the city that unless they have been specially detailed as officers or are on necessary business, that they remain off the public square and the principle streets, and especially to refrain from collecting in groups on or about the public square, for such gatherings, as you know, tend to arouse interest and excitement. Let us keep cool and be law abiding, and counsel each with the other against further agitation or discussion.

"The reputation of this city is at sake, and every good citizen is interested in maintaining and upholding the law. There is absolutely no further danger to life or property, if citizens regardless of color, will go about their business in a quiet way and refuse to be led into heated arguments or useless discussion of that which has already passed." B.E. Meyer, Mayor.

A grand jury was called and many witnesses were questioned. It was concluded that Horace Duncan and Fred Coker were not guilty of assaulting Mable Edwards and Charles Cooper. In the end, all charges concerning the mob hangings were dropped.

The front page news of this shocking atrocity did not linger long—a few days later San Francisco, California was shaken by a massive earthquake which stole the headlines all over the country. History, on the other hand, does not soon forget such outrage; it has a way of resurfacing again into the spotlight—and, while in the light, it can seize the opportunity to showcase the need for equality. It is a worthwhile lesson harvested along the traces of Ozarks past.

Vigilante Lynching in the "Queen City of the Ozarks"

Bibliography

Jackson, Rex T., *The Lynching of Horace Duncan, Fred Coker and Will Allen*, The Ozarks Reader Magazine, Vol. 9, No. 1, 2012.

Other Sources:
Joplin *Daily Globe*, April 15, 1906.
Springfield *Leader*, April 15, 1906.
Springfield *Republican*, April 15, 1906.

"BEFORE daybreak the tramp of horses reminded us our foragers were sallying forth. The red light from the countless campfires melted away as the dawn sole over the horizon, casting its wonderful gradations of light and color over the masses of sleeping soldiers, while the smoke of burning pine-knots befogged the chilly morning air. Then the bugles broke the impressive stillness, and the roll of drums was heard on all sides. Soon the scene was alive with blue coats and the hubbub of roll calling, cooking, and running for water to the nearest spring or stream. The surgeons looked to the sick and footsore, and weeded from the ambulances those who no longer needed to ride."

Marching Through Georgia and the Carolinas, Daniel Oakley, Captain, 2nd Massachusetts Volunteers, *Battles and Leaders of the Civil War*, The Century Company, 1887.

"THE COLUMN moved rapidly, considering the rough roads and the darkness, and from almost every wagon for many miles issued heart-rending wails of agony...Many of the wounded in the wagons had been without food for thirty-six hours. Their torn and bloody clothing, matted and hardened, was rasping the tender, inflamed, and still oozing wounds. Very few of the wagons had even a layer of straw in them, and all were without springs. The road was rough and rocky from the heavy washings of the preceding day. The jolting was enough to have killed strong men, if long exposed to it. From nearly every wagon as the teams trotted on, urged by whip and shouts, came...cries and shrieks...Some were simply moaning; some were praying, and others uttering the most fearful oaths and execrations that despair and agony could wring from them...."

The Confederate Retreat from Gettysburg, John D. Imboden, *Battles and Leaders of the Civil War*, Vol. 3, The Century Company, 1887.

Additional Illustrations

The likeness of Stand Watie carved in a monument at the Old Ridge-Polson Cemetery near Southwest City, Missouri, in Delaware County, Oklahoma.

The Cayuga Splitlog Mission built by Mathias Splitlog the "Millionaire Indian."

The Elkhorn Tavern at the Pea Ridge National Military Park, near Pea Ridge, Arkansas.

Historic marker just north of Commerce, Oklahoma, on Route 66, which commemorates Native Americans.

Historic marker at Van Buren, Arkansas, that commemorates the Butterfield Overland Mail Stagecoach Route.

Crouch Station Marker just north of Cassville, Missouri, that commemorates its place on the Butterfield Overland Mail Stagecoach Route.

Inside the War Eagle Mill, located east of Rogers, Arkansas.

The War Eagle River running past the War Eagle Mill.

Reenactment photo of Union soldiers taken at Carthage, Missouri.

Civil War reenactment photo taken near Bentonville, Arkansas.

Confederate soldiers at a Civil War reenactment in Cassville, Missouri.

Mural in Nevada, Missouri, of a steam-powered locomotive.

Index

Index

A

Adair County, Okla., 35
Asbury, Mo., 4
Allen, William, 126

B

Ballagh, W.T., 12
Baxter Springs, Kan., 5
Bellefontaine Cemetery, 96
Benna, Saturna "Doc", 20
Blackburn, Sylvanus, 92, 93
Blake, William "Tulsa Jack", 3, 78
Blow, Henry Taylor, 96, 99, 100, 101
Blunt, James G., 33, 38, 39, 40, 41, 99
Bolin, Alf, 27
Boudinot, Elias, 33, 34, 35
Broadwell, Dick, 78
Bronaugh, Mo., 14

C

Cabell, William L., 39, 41
Carthage, Mo., 71, 105, 109, 110, 119
Cassville, Mo., 85, 86, 120
Cayuga Springs, Okla., 20, 21, 22, 23
Chetopa, Kan., 13
Clay, Moses W., 20, 21, 22
Clifton, Dan "Dynamite Dick", 3, 78
Coffeyville, Kan., 2, 28, 78, 79
Coker, Fred, 124
Columbus, Kan., 5
Commerce, Okla., 5
Conrad, Joseph, 117, 118
Cooper, Douglas H., 36, 38, 40, 41, 98
Cox, George, 3
Crestline, Kan., 4
Curtis, Samuel R., 33, 36, 37, 86, 87, 93, 110, 111, 112

D

Dalton, Bill, 1, 27, 78
Dalton, Bob, 1, 27, 78
Dalton, Emmett, 1, 27, 78
Dalton, Grat, 1, 27, 78
Darst, W.J., 13
Daugherty, Roy "Arkansas Tom", 2, 3, 5, 6, 27, 63, 78
Davis, Jefferson, 41, 119
DeGraff, Tom, 4

"Devil's Promenade", 5
Dewey, Okla., 30
Doolin, William M. "Bill", 2, 3, 27, 76, 77, 78, 79, 80
Dorn, Earl Van, 33, 36, 37, 110, 111
Dover, Okla., 80
Duncan, Horace, 124

E

Eads, James B., 99, 100
Earp, Wyatt, 27
Eureka Springs, Ark., 80

F

Fairview, Mo., 3, 61, 62, 63
Floyd, "Pretty Boy", 61
Fort Smith, Ark., 21, 22
Foster, William, 97
Fremont, John C., 33

G

Galena, Kan., 5
Gano, Richard M., 33, 42
Gibson, William F., 5, 6
Gilyard, Thomas, 48, 49, 51
Goodman, Mo., 20, 22
Granby *Miner*, 100
Granby, Mo., 96, 97, 98, 99, 101, 102
Grounds, Bob, 79
Grove, Okla., 20
Guthrie, Okla., 77, 80

H

Harrison, Ark., 28, 31
Harrison *Times*, 26, 29
Hickok, James Butler "Wild Bill", 27
Hixson, John, 3
Hopkins, Mo., 74
Howell County *Gazette*, 55
Hueston, Ham, 3
Hueston, Tom, 3
Hurley, Mo., 64, 65

I

Ianson, M.A., 3
Ingalls, John J., 3
Ingalls, Okla., 79

J

Jackson, Claiborne Fox, 86, 117, 119
Jackson, Ernest J., 70, 72, 73, 74
Jackson, Eula, 70, 72, 73
James, Frank, 1, 27
James, Jesse, 1, 27
Jefferson City, Mo., 10
Joplin *Globe*, 5, 46, 47, 48, 49, 50, 51, 53, 122
Joplin, Mo., 47, 50, 62
Joplin *News Herald*, 4, 48, 50

K

Kansas City, Mo., 10

Keetsville (Washburn), Mo., 84, 85, 86, 87, 88, 110
Kel-Lake Motel, 70, 71, 72, 73, 74, 75
Keller, Henry, 3
Kellogg Lake, 71
Kelly, "Machine Gun", 61
Knob Noster, Mo., 10

L

Lee, Robert E., 43
Leslie, Theodore, 47, 48, 53
Loud, Gertrude, 8
Lyon, Nathaniel, 33, 65, 66, 117

M

Madsen, Chris, 80
Martin, Dimple, 57
Masterson, Bartholomew "Bat", 3, 27
Masterson, James, 3
Maysville, Ark., 35, 38
McCulloch, Ben, 33, 36, 110, 111
McIntosh, James, 36, 117
Mitchell, Laura B., 13
Montgomery, Samuel, 86, 87
Montserrat, Mo., 10
Muskogee, Okla., 30

N

Neosho *Daily Democrat*, 61, 62
Neosho, Mo., 21, 22, 116, 117, 118, 119, 120
Neosho *Times*, 18, 20, 21, 22, 23, 60, 61, 62, 63, 79, 82
Nevada *Daily*, 11, 14
Nevada, Mo., 12
Newcombe, "Bitter Creek", 3, 78
Newtonia, Mo., 37, 98, 113
New York *Times*, 100
Nix, E.D., 3

O

Oronogo, Mo., 3

P

Pea Ridge, Ark., 36, 108, 110, 114
Pensacola, Okla., 39
Pierce, Charley, 3, 79
Pike, Albert, 33, 36, 37, 110, 111, 112
Pleasant Hill, Mo., 10
Point Lookout, Mo., 31
Powers, Bill, 78
Preston, J.W., 10, 11
Price, Sterling, 33, 66, 110, 119, 120

Q

R

Raidler, Bill "Little", 78
Ream, Dicy, 8
Rentiesville, Okla., 39
Ridge, John, 34
Roberts, Doc, 3
Rogers, Ark., 92

Rome, Georgia, 33
Ross, John, 33, 35

S

Schofield, John M., 99
Sedalia, Mo., 10
Short, John, 65, 66, 67, 68
Lydia, Short, 65, 67, 68
Sigel, Franz, 33, 36, 110, 119
Simmons, Dell, 3
Sohn, Alf, 78
Southwest City *Enterprise*, 79
Southwest City, Mo., 32, 43, 44, 79, 80
Speed, Dick, 3
Splitlog, Mathias, 18, 19, 20, 21, 22, 23
Splitlog *Weekly*, 21
Springfield, Mo., 66, 68, 72, 104, 107, 110, 123, 124
Starr, Belle, 1, 27, 28
Starr, Henry, 27, 28, 29, 30, 31
Steel, Ike, 3
Stillwater, Okla., 3
St. Louis *Globe Democrat*, 100
St. Louis, Mo., 10, 11, 96, 99, 100
St. Louis World's Fair, 9, 10, 14
Swindle, George, 61

T

Thomas, Heck, 80
Tilghman, Bill, 80

U

V

VanDeventer, Len, 4, 6
Vickory, Madison, 97

W

Waightman, George "Red Buck", 3, 78
Warrensburg, Mo., 11, 14, 16
Warrensburg *Weekly Standard-Herald*, 10, 12, 16
Watie, Stand, 32, 33, 34, 35, 36, 39, 40, 41, 42, 43, 110
Watts, D.W., 13, 14
Watts, Okla., 35
West, Dick "Little", 78
West Plains, Mo., 54, 55, 58
West Plains *Weekly Quill*, 55
Wheaton, Mo., 3
White, Frank J., 105, 106
Wild Bunch, 3
Wiser, J.W., 56
Wright, Clark, 86, 87

X

Y

Yantis, Ole, 79
Younger, Bob, 1
Younger, Coleman, 1
Younger, Jim, 1

Z

Zagonyi, Charles, 104, 105, 106, 107

www.ingramcontent.com/pod-product-compliance
Lightning Source LLC
Chambersburg PA
CBHW050639160426
43194CB00010B/1741